POMERANIANS
AND
THE POMERANIAN

Pomeranian
Total Guide

POMERANIANS, POMERANIAN DOGS, POMERANIAN
PUPPIES, POMERANIAN TRAINING, POMERANIAN BREEDERS,
POMERANIAN HEALTH, & MUCH MORE COVERED!

Mark Manfield

© DYM Worldwide Publishers

The Pomeranian is a robust, spunky, intelligent toy breed. Its charming personality and teddy-bear-like appearance make the Pomeranian one of the most popular purebred dogs in the world!

Published by DYM Worldwide Publishers, 2018.

ISBN: 978-1-911355-76-2

DYM Worldwide Publishers takes no responsibility for, and will not be liable for, the websites being temporarily or being removed from the Internet. The accuracy and completeness of the information provided herein and opinions stated herein are not guaranteed or warranted to produce any particular results, and the advice or strategies, contained herein may not be suitable for every individual. The author, publisher, distributors, and/or affiliates shall not be liable for any loss incurred as a consequence of the use and application, directly or indirectly of any information presented in this work. This publication is designed to provide information regarding the subject matter covered. The information included in this book has been compiled to give an overview of the topics covered. The information contained in this book has been compiled to provide an overview of the subject. It is not intended as medical advice and should not be construed as such. For a firm diagnosis of any medical conditions, you should consult a doctor or veterinarian (as related to animal health). The writer, publisher, distributors, and/or affiliates of this work are not responsible for any damages or negative consequences following any of the treatments or methods highlighted in this book.

Website links are for informational purposes only and should not be seen as a personal endorsement; the same applies to any products or services mentioned in this work. The reader should also be aware that although the web links included were correct at the time of writing they may become out of date in the future. Any pricing or currency exchange rate information was accurate at the time of writing but may become out of date in the future. The Author, Publisher, distributors, and/or affiliates assume no responsibility for pricing and currency exchange rates mentioned within this work.

Table of Contents

Introduction to the Pomeranian

You have decided a Pomeranian Dog just may be the perfect canine companion for your family. You are not alone. This delightful breed has been a favorite of families since the 18th century. It is little wonder Pomeranians (also called "Poms") consistently rank in the top 20 most favorite breeds among purebred dogs recognized by kennel club registries. This tiny, energetic dog is all heart. Fiercely loyal to its humans the Pomeranian is recognized as being playful, entertaining, loving, outgoing, and very intelligent. Factor in a relatively long lifespan, fun-loving disposition, and an adorable teddy bear appearance and you have a dog that is simply irresistible. Properly trained, a fashionable little Pom will make a polite, pleasing, perfect companion for his entire life.

CHAPTER 1

The History of the Pomeranian Dog

The Pomeranian, also known as "Pom," "Pom Pom," and "Tumbleweed," is a member of the Spitz family of canines. Cousins of the Pomeranian include; the Akita, Norwegian Elkhound, Welsh Corgi, and various sled dogs such as the Alaskan Malamute, Siberian Husky, Canadian Eskimo Dog, and the Greenland Dog. Spitz Dogs were developed for hunting, herding, and pulling sleds. They were valued as strong, powerful, muscular dogs with a solid, devoted work ethic. Through selective breeding practices, smaller Spitz dogs were cultivated including the Fox Spitz, Welsh Corgi, and Pomeranian.

Pomeranian Dogs are believed to be descendants of the Nordic White Spitz Sled Dog.

Characteristically, Spitz dogs are identified by a long, thick coat (often white), pointed ears, and a sharp muzzle. Many German-speaking countries continue to use the name *Zwergspitz* ("Dwarf Spitz") to identify the Pomeranian Dog.

What is the Origin of the Pomeranian?

The name *"Pomeranian"* originates from the Central European region of Germany/Poland known as "Pomerania." The breed is actually believed to have evolved through various areas of Europe with no relation to Pomerania and is historically identified by several different names. In 1788, naturalist Johann Friedrich Gmelin documented the development of the Spitz Dog in

Systema Naturale 13th Edition. There, and in various other periodicals, the breed is identified as *"Canis Pomeramus."*

It wasn't until the marriage of Charlotte of Mecklenburg-Strelitz and King George III of England that the Pomeranian became a noteworthy breed. Queen Charlotte brought her beloved "Wolf dogs" to England in 1761, and they were firmly established members of the royal court. The new queen's precious pets were imported from a breeder located in Pomerania, and she called her dogs *"Pomeranians."*

What were Pomeranian Dogs Bred for?

Dogs in the 17th century were used as working stock and few if any were housed as pets. Queen Charlotte's passion for her dogs soon established an acceptable tradition for the country's royals and commoners alike. Pomeranians (as well as other small dogs) became a familiar fixture in homes. Many paintings from the time feature Pomeranians as treasured family members. They are among the first canine breed developed specifically for human companionship.

In the latter part of the 18th century, the Pomeranian gained international recognition. In 1859, the city of Newcastle held the first English dog show in conjunction with their renowned cattle show. The dog exhibition was a big hit with patrons. Around the beginning of the 1900s dog shows were held in various countries attracting hundreds of entries and paying visitors. The canine competitions became much-anticipated events drawing the attention of the privileged and the poor alike. Dog shows, in general, are credited with making dog fancying fashionable and respectable throughout Europe.

A Pomeranian Fox Dog won the non-sporting, foreign dog class at Manchester's Belle Vue Zoo show in 1861, and interest in the breed was immediate. By 1963, there were enough Pomeranian Dogs entered in London's Great International Dog Show to secure a class of their own. The English Kennel Club formally entered the breed in the registry book as *"Pomeranian"* in 1891.

Pomeranian Dogs in History

Queen Charlottes' granddaughter, Queen Victoria, inherited her grandmother's affection for the adorable Pomeranian. She brought her first Poms to Windsor Castle in 1888. At one time, during Victoria's reign, there were 35 Pomeranians in the royal kennel. The Queen's interest in the breed extended to show competition and a royal breeding program. Queen Victoria was recognized as a top breeder, and she developed a variety of colors of Pomeranian as well promoting the line of "toy" dogs.

Queen Victoria is credited with making the breed extremely popular by displaying her dogs with constant public exposure. She rarely traveled without her Pomeranian pets. Her royal train included a special compartment for the dogs. They even had a security detail assigned to their care and protection. Queen Victoria requested her favorite Pom "Turi" be brought to her deathbed. She died with her faithful companion by her side in 1901.

The concept of companion pet dogs flourished throughout Europe and into the United States. The breed "Pomeranian" was officially recognized by the American Kennel Club (AKC) in 1888. The first Pomeranian breed show was held at the Waldorf Astoria Hotel in New York City in 1911. It took 100-years for a Pomeranian to win the prestigious "Best in Show" title at the famous Westminster Kennel Club in Madison Square Garden. "Great Elms Prince Charming II" captured the coveted crown in 1988 along with the admiration of some 7,500 spectators in attendance.

Historical records, letters, and paintings are dotted with accounts of loyal Pomeranians. In addition to Queen Charlotte and Queen Victoria, Poms were members of other royal courts including those of Marie Antoinette (1755-1793), and Empress Josephine of France (1763-1814), the wife of Napoleon I.

The famous composer Wolfgang Amadeus Mozart wrote an aria to immortalize his cherished Pomeranian named Pimperl. Michaelango's little Pom is believed to have perched on a satin pillow while watching his master paint the Sistine Chapel. Church reformist, Martin Luther, wrote about his much-loved Pomeranian Belferlein. Then there is Sir Issac Newtons's Pomeranian, "Diamond," who is believed to have tipped over a candle causing the fire that destroyed much of the eminent scientist's life's work of papers resulting in Newton's nervous breakdown.

Charles Darwin owned a Pom named Snow. The magician Harry Houdini had a Pomeranian he named Charlie. Two Pomeranians were rescued with their owners from the sinking of the Titanic. Poms "Sweet Pea" and "Edmond" were adored by their owner, the American "King" Elvis Presley.

*Pomeranian Dogs are travel-ready
companions for jet-setting lifestyles.*

Pomeranian Dogs in Popular Culture

Owning a fashionable, adorable, paparazzi magnet pooch is more trendy today than ever. Many celebrities find the go-everywhere Pomeranian a comforting accessory for their jet-setting lifestyles. Among the *"Poministas"* of the current popular culture

- Nicole Ritchie
- Eva Longoria
- Kelly Osbourne

- Gavin Rossdale
- LeeAnn Rimes
- Keanu Reeves
- Kate Hudson
- Britney Spears
- Rhianna
- Gwen Stefani
- Jane Fonda
- Sylvester Stallone.

A few Pomeranian Dogs have achieved celebrity status on their own merit by appearing in movies, television shows, and in various media advertisements. The movies *To Die For, Dumb and Dumber, Harlem Nights, X-Files, Cadillac Man,* and *Quigley* all feature an adorable, little Pomeranian star.

Cindy William's Pom "Phoebe" costars in William's Jenny Craig advertisements. "Shashi" is the canine actor featured in the movies *Quigley* and *Chasing Papi.*

Jiff a handsome, multitalented Pom appeared in Banana Republic and Target television commercials and held a starring role in *The Adventure of Bailey: A Night in Cowtown.* Don't let Jiff's pretty boy face fool you. He is also an accomplished athlete. Jiff was entered in the *Guinness Book of World Record* for running 10 meters in 6.56 seconds on his HIND legs! The City of Los Angeles, California honored Jiff's many exceptional feats by officially naming August 20, 2014 "Jiff Day!"

Given the popularity of the Pomeranian, there is a good chance one or more of the glamorous divas will appear strutting with her famous human, peeking out of a designer purse, or tucked securely in the arms of a rich and famous owner. Pom's love the camera and the feeling appears to be mutual. Ever ready to strike a pose often upstaging their human "A-list" celebrity, a well-groomed Pom Pom seems to be communicating, "Don't hate me because I'm beautiful!"

Pomeranian Historic Records

The Pomeranian/Spitz ancestors were much larger dogs compared to today's standards. Early breeding records indicate an average weight of between 20 and 30 pounds (9 – 13.5 kilograms), and a standing height of about 18 inches (45.7 centimeters) at the withers for an adult Pomeranian.

Queen Victoria's first Pom "Marco," imported from Italy was reported to be a small Pomeranian. Weighing 12 pounds (5.4 kgs.), Marco was a crowd favorite at dog shows and consistently won top honors. Queen Victoria's preference for the smaller-sized dogs influenced her breeding program and ultimately the popularity of the more diminutive Poms.

The World's Smallest Pomeranian

Selective breeding and buyers demand resulted in establishing the Pomeranian as one of the smallest purebred dogs recognized by kennel clubs. The smallest Pomeranian of modern record is a male named Mr. Amazing. The little guy weighed a mere 11.6 ounces and stood 2.5 inches tall at the withers. He caught the attention of the hotel heiress Paris Hilton who paid an impressive

$13,000 (10559.900 EUR) for the 5-month-old, all white puppy in 2014. Mr.Amazing not only holds the record for being the smallest Pomeranian in the world; he is also the most expensive.

Pomeranian Breed Popularity Ranking

The Pomeranian is among the world's most popular purebred breed. Since 1930, kennel club registrations in the UK and America ranked the Pom in the top ten percent of breeds. After World War II, Pomeranian registrations declined to a slightly lower ranking. In 1994 the little dogs returned to the top-ten spot, holding a place in the highest percentile every consecutive year since.

European Pomeranian and American Pomeranian – What's the Difference?

The Pomeranian is a small, sturdy, active dog of Nordic descent. Developed in several countries of Europe the appearance of the modern Pomeranian is the result of selective breeding processes primarily concentrated in Great Britain during the latter part of the 18th century.

Characteristic differences in the "European Pomeranian" and "American Pomeranian" as defined by today's breed club standards are minor. To the average observer, a purebred Pom looks much the same as any other purebred Pom despite the country of breeding. There are subtle differences in individual size (by a pound or two), and the broad color variations of the dogs are obvious.

Basic descriptions of the classic toy Pomeranian include a prominent short, compact, fox-like appearance. The Pom's coat is long, fluffy and may be one of several different colors or blend of colors. The tail is a full, feathered plume and the eyes are dark brown or black, round, alert, and expressive. Two areas of discernment in club standards are the eyes and body weight. The American Kennel Club cites any blue coloring of the eye as a fault. The AKC weight standard for conformation is 3 pounds to 7 pounds for dogs and bitches. The UK Kennel Club establishes 4 pounds to 4 ½ pounds (1.8 - 2 kgs.) for dogs and 4 ½ to 5 ½ pounds (2 – 2.5 kgs.) for bitches, as standard.

CHAPTER 2

What Should You Know About Owning a Pomeranian? Pom Pom 101

Pomeranians are intelligent, energetic, loyal, proud dogs who will do nearly anything to please their human. A confident, natural entertainer, with a gorgeous appearance the little Pom typically does exceptionally well in the show ring, but the appeal doesn't end with dog shows. Poms possess a wide range of abilities including obedience trials and agility races. They are excellent performers preferred by animal trainers for their intelligence and ability to learn. Poms are also trained as therapy dogs, comfort dogs, and specialty service dogs. Believe it, or not the tiny Pomeranian makes a terrific WATCHDOG!

A captivating interest in the Pomeranian led you to research the breed to determine if it is just right for your family. Good job! The gorgeous balls of fluff make wonderful, versatile family pets. They are small enough to fit in a backpack but are full of personality. Make no mistake, adopting a Pomeranian, or any dog represents a lifetime commitment. Determining the appropriate time involved in raising a puppy, versus choosing an adult dog, is also a consideration. In this chapter, we will discuss the basic needs and requirements of Pomeranian ownership.

Pomeranians as Pets – What Kind of Home is Best Suited?

Selecting a Pomeranian as a pet goes beyond an appreciation of the exquisite appearance and dynamic personality of the dog. Understanding the traits of the breed prepares potential owners for the commitment of training, grooming, socializing, and health care. Breed knowledge also provides an awareness of the Pom's less desirable tendencies and prepares his owners to live with them.

The physical environment (home) required for the comfort and health of a Pomeranian is fairly simple. A Pom can live just about anywhere his or her humans do. The small, robust Pom is an ideal pet for apartment dwelling. They are typically very active indoors and can get adequate exercise without a yard. The major considerations for this little dog's comfort, are appropriate temperature controls to prevent overheating or chilling, and loads of love and attention.

Is the Pomeranian a Rare Breed?

The term "rare breed" is used among dog circles to identify a dog that is purebred but existing in very small numbers. Some breeds are so rare that there are a very few specimens left, even in their homeland of origin. Dedicated breeders have worked diligently to establish sound, "typey," beautiful Pomeranians for generations. Their efforts, along with buyer demands have made the Pom one of the most popular dog breeds in the world. By definition, the Pomeranian is not considered a rare breed. While the Pomeranian breed is not considered rare, there are coat color classifications of Pomeranians that are rare.

Purebred Pomeranian Standards

There are many discussions and confusions regarding the purpose of a "breed standard." Many buyers just want a good pet; they aren't interested in showing or breeding their dog they simply want a good companion, so why the concern about a breed standard?

A breed standard is an important set of guidelines established to evaluate a breed's external, observable qualities. Specifically, breed standards define the acceptable qualities of appearance, temperament, type, and movement. It is the adherence to the breed standard that breeders strive for to produce their lines, and it is the standards that buyers should look for when selecting a quality, purebred Pomeranian (or any other breed).

Pomeranian General Appearance

What does a Pomeranian puppy look like? Few living animals on earth are cuter than a puppy – any puppy. Factor in the offspring of what is quite possibly the most beautiful dog in the world and you will have the description of something that is simply irresistible – the Pomeranian puppy!

Newborn Poms look pretty much like any other newborn dog. They are covered with a fine, downy fuzz and may be any number of colors. The legendary Pomeranian tail on the baby is little more than a thin stem. Newborns often look so much alike most breeders will attach a band or ribbon to each puppy as they are born, to identify and track the individual babies. A Pomeranian dam may give birth to 1 to 5 puppies in a litter. The newborn's eyes are closed for several days, and they weigh just a few ounces.

A few days after birth the puppy's eyes open and they crawl on their stomachs in search of a food source – their mother. As they grow, a down-like fur begins to form their baby coats. It is common for a puppy to be born with a dark skin only to end up with a light coat as an adult, or a light-skinned pup may have a dark coat. Between 12 and 20 weeks of age, Pomeranian puppies lose the baby coat and begin a stage fondly referred to as the "puppy uglies." True to the name the pups in this stage are very raggedy, scraggly looking and well…ugly! The coat becomes a thin, sparse, spiky, fur covering. It is necessary to lose the baby coat entirely before the adult coat can fully establish. Some Poms completely shed and regrow their fur several times during their growth periods. It usually takes four to six months for the hair to regrow and up to two years for the luxurious, adult Pomeranian coat to totally develop.

What does an adult Pomeranian Dog look like? A fully-grown Pomeranian is still a "toy-sized" dog ideally weighing between 3 and 7 pounds (1.8 to 3 kgs). The wedge-shaped head is proportionate to the body. Almond-shaped eyes are very dark, bright, and expressive. A fine, straight muzzle and sharp, erect ears give the Pom its classic "foxlike" appearance. The nose is dark, but the color may vary slightly depending on the coat color. The Pomeranians distinctively feathered tail lies straight and flat over the back. The other distinguishing factor to the Pom's appearance is the abundant, thick, double coat. The outer coat is straight, silky and long and the undercoat is thick and short. A thicker growth area around the neck and chest creates a "mane-like" mantle. Pomeranian coats come in a wide variety of acceptable colors and blends of colors and markings.

Pomeranian Growth – How Fast Does a Pomeranian Puppy Grow?

A healthy, vital Pomeranian puppy will grow from a helpless neonate unable to see, hear, or walk, and completely dependent on the mother to a fully grown, independent, agile, sexually mature dog in about twelve months. Small breeds like the Pom reach maturity much faster than larger breed dogs. Pomeranian puppies like all other dogs have predictable stages of growth and development.

Pomeranian Adults – How large can a Pomeranian grow? In the purebred dog world SIZE MATTERS. Dedicated Pomeranian breeders have worked diligently for more than a century to establish a standard of size for the breed. According to kennel club guidelines, an adult Pomeranian should stand between 8 and 11 inches (20.32 to 27.94 centimeters) tall at the withers (shoulder) when measured in a standing position. The exact size of an adult Pom is largely determined by genetics.

Pomeranian Adults – How heavy can a Pomeranian get? In 1960, the accepted purebred Pomeranian weight adopted by most kennel clubs for was defined as 3 to 7 pounds (1.25 to 3.15 kilograms). Some modern Pomeranians will reach an adult size of only 2 pounds (.9 kilograms). These tiny specimens are nicknamed "flyweights." At the other end of the scale some Poms nicknamed "throwbacks" may get as large as 12 to 18 pounds (5.4 to 8.1 kilograms). Breeders who fail to follow best practice procedures may produce adult Pomeranian smaller or much larger than the "standard." The official standard of any kennel club clearly states that dogs who are too big or too small should never be bred.

The Pomeranian is one of the most popular breeds in the world, but it is not a rare breed.

The Pomeranian's Tail

The lovely plumed tail of the Pomeranian is among the breed's most distinctive physical feature. The first Pomeranian/Spitz dogs' tail curled tightly over the back. As the Pom evolved, the tail progressively grew straighter. The modern Pom's tail is feathered and full. It lies on the top of the back with long hair fanning out often reaching the dog's sides.

The Pomeranian's Ears

The Pom's ears are mounted high on the top of the head. They are small and triangular shaped with firm points that remain erect. In show judging, it is the position rather than the size and shape of the ear that is considered first. The range of ear size is apparent in the breed. Some Pomeranians have very, very tiny ears (most valued in a show dog) others have larger ears when compared to the size of the dog. Ear size is a genetic determination and buyers should examine both the sire and dam of any litter to predict the ear size of the offspring.

The Pomeranian's Muzzle

Kennel club's standards define the Pomeranian muzzle as being rather short and straight. The length of the muzzle to the skull should be a proper ratio of the length of muzzle to the skull (⅓ to ⅔) and should not produce an excessively elongated nose. The breed's resemblance to a fox is especially noticeable in the face which should be enhanced with an alert, bright, engaging, inquisitive expression.

The Pomeranian Coat of Many Colors — What Color Coat is Acceptable?

The most common color associated with the Pomeranian is the classic pale orange or "red" shade. Early Pom/Spitz were pure white dogs. Queen Victoria's earliest Pom was a small red dog, and that color became very popular by the end of the 19th century. Pioneering efforts in the selective breeding process introduced many different color coats in association with the Pomeranian. Astute breeders, in the attempt to produce a consistently smaller dog, recognized white dogs produced bigger puppies regardless of the size of the sire and dam.

Today, the Pomeranian is accepted in the widest variety of colors of any breed. The AKC lists 18 different colors as standard including; white, black, brown, red, orange, cream, blue, and sable. Eight patterns or markings of black and tan, brown and tan, cream and white, spotted, brindle or any combinations are also acceptable. The most common Pom colors are orange, black, or cream and white. Due to the vast number of colors in the Pomeranian bloodline, it is rare to produce certain solid color Poms.

Black Pomeranian Dog — True black is one of the rare coat colors of the breed. Black Poms will not only have black fur, but they will have black skin pigmentation, eye rims, lips, nose, and paw pads. Pomeranian puppies may be born with dark pigmentation leading their breeder to identify them as "black" when in fact they may flash other colors as the adult coat comes in. Pomeranians with a black coat mixed with even a hint of any other color are considered "mismarked" or tri-colored.

White Pomeranian Dog — Pomeranians were developed from Nordic white Spitz sled-dogs. There was a time Pomeranians weighed between 20 and 30 pounds, and they were all white. Years of successful selective breeding produced the modern standard 5 to 7-pound Pom and also resulted in developing the broadest range of colors among purebred dogs. The practice introduced many different colors in the gene pool and made achieving the all-white Pom a slow, difficult task today. To be officially registered "white," the coat must not contain any other tint or coloring including cream or yellow. In fact, the designation goes further than the eye can see, a registered "white" Pomeranian must not have shown any other color in their gene pool for at least 5 generations!

Careful consideration of the sire and dam is necessary to produce a quality coat as well as a white Pomeranian. Breeding two all-white mates often produce a "throwback" (puppy larger than standard size) even if both parents are within the standard. The quality of the coat of the offspring is also affected when two white dogs are bred.

A White Pomeranian puppy may keep a white coat for several months, only to change color and end up developing a cream, yellow, or "parti-color" adult coat. Since most pups are sold well before the adult coat establishes, experienced breeders have learned to depend on the area behind the puppy's ear or on the hocks to predict coat color. Any shading of these areas and the Pom will not have an all-white adult coat.

Brown Pomeranian Dog — A true brown Pomeranian is also something of a rarity as most dark dogs have some other colors in their coat. It is also a difficult color to define as there are several ranges of brown including chocolate, beaver, and dark cream. Brown Poms are so dark it is difficult to determine if they are brown or black. It often takes comparing a hair from a black Pomeranian and a brown Pom to determine the correct colors.

Orange Pomeranian Dog — Orange is the most popular of all Pomeranian coat designations. The intensity of the orange color may range from deep rust, bright gold to a light honey color.

Orange Pomeranian newborns are frequently a dark sable color or born with very pale almost white pigmentation. Regardless of the pigmentation, the coat color will become orange as the puppy matures.

Chocolate Pomeranian Dog — The designation of a "Chocolate" Pomeranian captures a wide-range of colors, including brown. It is one of the most confusing color registrations for breeders, buyers, and the casual observer. In determining the proper coat color, it may require evaluating the eye rims, paw pads, lips, and most importantly the nose. If a Pom has a coat color ranging from light cream to a dark brown but has a black nose, that dog is officially considered a cream Pomeranian.

A chocolate Pomeranian has dark chocolate brown eye rims, paw pads, lips, and nose. Color variations may range from cream to a dark, almost black coat. Regardless of the depth of color, the pigmentation must be dark brown to garner a chocolate Pomeranian registry. A chocolate Pomeranian puppy can only be produced by mating two chocolate mates carrying the chocolate color gene. A typical litter for a Pom is 2-4 offspring, and it is possible that breeding two chocolate Poms may not produce chocolate puppy, such are the genetics.

Red Pomeranian Dog — While most red Poms are actually orange by definition, red is an accepted color of a Pomeranian coat. As with other colors, the red coat of an adult Pom will change with maturity. Additionally, a dark chocolate Pom's coat will often throw a red tint, making an almost mahogany hue (caused by sun exposure).

Remember, the Pomeranian breed is famous for changing coat colors. A red Pomeranian puppy may turn any number of shades, tones, or even mixed colors over a lifetime. For this reason, a reputable breeder would never "guarantee" the color of a puppy.

Cream Pomeranian Dog — The cream color designation of Pomeranian can vary considerably. The coloring can be very light, almost white with shade gradients to a darker brown. It is necessary to evaluate skin pigmentation to determine the correct color designation. A cream Pom will have black eye rims, nose, lips, and paw pad pigmentation (whereas the chocolate Pom will feature brown points). Black may also show behind the ears and hocks.

Buyers seeking an all-white Pom should beware – a cream Pomeranian puppy is often sold as "white" because the coloring isn't apparent until after the adult coat is grown.

Blue Pomeranian Dog — A Blue Pomeranian Dog's coat may appear black, but if the skin carries a blue tint the dog is genetically blue. The eyelids, nose, ear points, lips, and paw pads are all blue. Blue is actually a diluted black color gene. The dark fur of a Blue Pomeranian Dog may appear dull and lack the sheen of a Black Pom. Blue Poms are also commonly born with blue eyes (considered a fault in the AKC breed standard).

It is often difficult to designate a newborn's color before the coat and skin mature. The best test to determine the true Blue Pomeranian Puppy is to inspect the nose for a blue tint carefully.

Lavender Pomeranian Dogs — Lavender is among the rarest and exotic of Pomeranian coat colors. It is not a recognized color by kennel clubs, and Lavender Poms must be registered as cream, beaver or another color, depending on the hue. The lavender tint shows as a light purple in the Pom's coat. Also considered "lilac," the color is most likely the result of a diluted blue or beaver gene.

Making the Mark – What are Acceptable Pomeranian Markings?

Brindle Pomeranian Dog – A Brindle Pomeranian may be any number of accepted base colors including the most popular orange, red, or gold. Visible striped cross patterns in the coat designate a Brindle Pomeranian Dog. The stripes may appear in conjunction with other marking patterns, such as a Parti or Black and Tan (the stripes will only be apparent in the tan areas). The undercoat and eyelids, ears, nose, and paw pad points should reflect the correct color for the base coat.

Brindle Pomeranian Puppy's stripes often extend the entire length of the body or may appear as dorsal stripes instead. The coat color may change, and the fur grows longer as the adult coat is established, so the brindle stripes may become broken in the mature Brindle Pomeranian Dog's coat. Many adult Brindle Pomeranian Dog's only show their stripe across the saddle (back).

Beaver Pomeranian Dog – The Beaver Pomeranian Dog is another interesting color designation. The coat color is in the brown range; cream, dark brown, tan, or chocolate. The official determination of "Beaver" is made based on the color of the skin pigmentation. A Beaver Pomeranian Dog will have beaver colored skin points, eyes, ears, paw pads, and lips.

A Beaver Pomeranian Puppy may show lighter pigmentation on skin points at birth especially on the nose.

Parti-color Pomeranian Dog –Parti-color Pomeranian Dogs are most remarkable as the markings on each individual dog are unique. The rare aspect of a parti coat makes this little Poms very coveted. Parti markings consist of two colors, and the AKC standard suggests that one of the two colors, should be white.

Parti-color Pomeranian puppies may be difficult to identify until the puppy coat has transitioned, and the adult coat is established. Even the percentage of the different coat colors morph, as the dog matures.

There are three different types of Parti-color Pomeranians, with white being one of the colors defined by the AKC and other kennel club standards:

1. The **Extreme Piebald Parti Pomeranian** features white as the majority of the coat color, and the tip of the tail is also white.
2. The **Piebald Parti Pomeranian** is approximately 50% white and 50% another color.
3. The **Irish Marked Pomeranian Dog** will show other colors in addition to required white. Small patches of white may appear on the ears, paws, and chest.

Mask Pomeranian Dog – The designation of "Mask Pomeranian Dog" represents a Pom that develops a mask-like mark across the muzzle and around the eyes. Many masks are black, but any color may be present.

A Pomeranian newborn may not develop the clear marking of the mask until the adult coat is formed. A mask that is clearly formed may fade, or the definition may break, as the pup's adult coat develops.

Merle Pomeranian Dog – The combination of colors that make a "Merle" Pomeranian Dog are varied. The base coat of a Merle Pomeranian is usually a solid red, brown, or black with mottled patches of blue, red, or grey. The speckled effect resembles freckles. In addition to the color of the coat, the "merle" gene contributes to pigmentation of the eyes, nose, and paw pads.

While the Merle Pomeranian is considered somewhat rare and consequently sought-after, there are health concerns associated with the gene. Merle Poms are prone to experience deafness, eye defects, and sterility. The AKC and other kennel clubs disqualify Pomeranians with light blue eyes, blue marbled eyes, or blue flecked eyes from conformation.

Merle Pomeranian Puppies may be identified by carefully examining the nose and paw pads. A Merle puppy's pigmentation will often be pink with black spots.

Sable Pomeranian Dog – A Sable Pomeranian Dog will have a solid base coat. Sable is defined as a coat that shows dark tips on the guard hair. A Sable Pomeranian may be any number of different color variations.

It is difficult to predict a Sable Pomeranian Puppy. If one of the parents is a Sable Pomeranian Dog, there is a good chance one or more offspring will produce a sable coat. The dark tips on the hair do not become apparent, until the pup grows through the "puppy uglies" stage, and develops his adult coat.

What is the Pomeranian Temperament?

The beautiful Pomeranian Dog as a breed is intelligent, curious, animated, energetic, and completely loveable. The total package of the Pom is undeniably attractive, and it makes this breed one of the most popular companion pets in the world. With all that great fluff and favor comes a few less than less-than-desirable breed characteristics.

Poms love to bark, a good trait for an alarm dog, but the fuss may be problematic in some environments. The barking can be such a nuisance that it is one of the top reasons cited for a Pom's rehoming, or its surrender to a shelter. Even calmer, less vocal Pomeranians have that common high pitched yap. If a quiet, sedate, serene dog is what you prefer, it may be good to find a breed with much less to say.

Pomeranians are independent, proud, self-possessed dogs, wholly loyal to their humans. They also have the reputation of being strong-willed, with a mind of their own. It takes a confident, disciplined owner/trainer to help a Pomeranian become a well-behaved family member.

The bond Pomeranian Dogs hold for their humans knows no bounds. They want to be with you all the time. What could be wrong with that kind of unconditional love? Poms often suffer separation anxiety. Separation anxiety is a condition of nervous alarm when the object of desire is removed. Pomeranian owners must establish themselves as the pack leader, and promote the dog's security, within the family pack.

The little, teddy-bear of a pup loves to be loved. Nothing makes a Pom happier than sitting on his human's lap and being adored. The affection is addictive, and most Pomeranian owners are happy to provide ample attention. The demand can become excessive and annoying. It can also lead to jealousy and other territorial tendencies.

What do you need to know about Pomeranian Behavior?

Most Poms are friendly, people-centric dogs by nature. Some are shy around strangers and suspicious in unfamiliar environments. Owners must socialize their Pomeranians on a regular basis to encourage their natural friendly dispositions and to prevent undesirable fearful, guarded, anxious behaviors.

The irresistible Pom is very bright with a mind of its own. They are not typically submissive, and they can be very obstinate. To avoid being manipulated by the dog's stubborn, inflexible nature, owners must adopt a consistent, firm posture when working with their Pomeranian.

One of the most charming and frustrating aspects of the Pomeranian is the constant desire to vocalize – in other words, they bark, and bark, and bark. Barking is a communication means for all dogs, some more habitually than others. Poms take the trait to an entirely new level. Their alert, inquisitive character generates a hyperawareness of their surroundings. Poms consider it their mission to make the household aware of every sound, sight, scent, or subtle shift in the universe.

Pomeranians are notoriously difficult to housebreak. Their tiny bodies will fit beneath furniture, hide in draperies, under beds, and behind doors. They can find very inconspicuous, discrete places to 'go potty.' Housebreaking any puppy depends on immediate correction, but you can't correct what you don't see. Most toy dogs, including Pomeranian Dogs, require consistent crate training to achieve successful housebreaking results.

There are several reasons families with small children are discouraged from considering adding a Pomeranian Dog to the household. One of the primary reasons is the breed's tendency to be territorial and possessive of food, toys, or favorite people. They love attention and will demonstrate jealous behaviors. Children who do not understand or respect the Pom's boundaries may be growled at, snapped at, or bitten.

Napoleon Complex – Pomeranian Dog owners will tell you the breed is big on personality. That enormous personality can lead to undesirable traits if it manifests in assertive, destructive, belligerent behavior. The term Napoleon Complex is commonly used to categorize the excessive behavior of a small dog that is apparently overcompensating for size, by being inappropriately aggressive. Named for the "small-in-stature," French emperor Napoleon Bonaparte, the Napoleon Complex is also called the "small dog syndrome." Many small dogs both purebred and mixed breeds have the tendency to exhibit a Napoleon Complex, and the Pomeranian Dog is certainly no exception. It should be noted there is a difference between a Pom that is spunky and confident and a dog with "small dog syndrome." Symptoms of Napoleon Complex include: not following learned commands, exercising territorial tendencies over certain areas or belongings, demonstrating food aggression, and acting out by growling, snapping, or even biting. Consistent training and firm but patient handling, are essential to overcome a Napoleon Complex and develop a confident, approachable, well-adjusted Pom.

Pomeranian Life Expectancy – How long will a Pomeranian Live?

A positive and important aspect of adding a Pomeranian to your family is the breed's relatively long lifespan. Many healthy Poms live to an age of 15 or 16 years. Thanks to medical advancements, improvements in nutrition, and better breeding practices there are many reports of Pomeranians living 20 years or longer. The biggest health issues with the Pom's aging process – barring injuries caused by accidents and trauma – is the onset of arthritis.

Pomeranian Guard Dog – Is the Pom the Right Breed to Guard your Family?

Many organizations cite ownership of a dog as one of the best deterrents of home burglaries. The idea of a 5-pound ball of fur attacking a big, strapping burglar may seem humorous but it is the bark and not the bite that is important, and it is recognized the Pomeranian has a world-class bark!

The observant, aware, fearless Pom may not be effective in a fight, but he will certainly sound the alarm if danger approaches. In most cases, the incessant barking is all it takes to scare away even the biggest intruder.

Pomeranian Show Dog – How to Prepare Your Pomeranian for the Show Ring

Pomeranians have been successful show competitors since their recognition as companion pets. The first recorded Pomeranian "Spitz" Dog to compete in a dog show was in 1861. A gorgeous Pom named The Sable Mite captured the Best of Show at the UK's famed Crufts Show in 1905. The same dog took home the crown in 1907. The first Pomeranian to win at the prestigious US Westminster was Great Elms Prince Charming II who was named the top dog in 1988.

Pomeranians are a crowd favorite on dog show circuits around the world, and indeed dog shows are credited with driving the popularity of the breed. Shows are considered a noble sport for man and beast. They offer valuable educational resources about the breed, information about breeders, and they establish the physical standard for all kennel club sanctioned purebred dogs.

It should be anticipated that obtaining a show-quality Pomeranian requires more research, planning, and cost than is expected with locating a companion pet. Owning a successful show dog also involves extra training, time, personal effort, and ultimately translates to additional expense. Ambitious owners planning to embark on a show career should attend shows and identify breeders who have produced multiple champions to find a good show potential pup. Most reputable breeders welcome questions about show quality Poms and will even offer to mentor their client for the life of the dog.

Competition shows for dogs are not limited to conformation. Sanctioned contests are open for agility, obedience, rally, diving, there are even freestyle dog dancing competitions. The "show-quality" designation of Pomeranian Puppies references the revered conformation showing.

Conformation is the event that evaluates a purebred dog's proximity to the breed standard. Experienced, educated, certified judges measure the competitor's close representation to the kennel club's breed standard (Best of Breed title). In the first qualifying pass of conformation, dogs are evaluated by gender and age against other dogs of the same breed. The ultimate winner of the breed class progresses to represent the breed in a group contest (Best of Group). In this meet, all of the winners of the various breeds within a group are judged. Finally, the Best of Group winner goes to the Championship competition, and the winner is named Best of Show. It is the canine equivalent of a beauty contest and an exciting, fun sport for competitors and spectators alike.

To win a world-class dog show like Crufts or Westminster, you must have the "A-Team" consisting of an exemplary dog and a handler with top handling skills. Showing for conformation requires a significant commitment of time, money, and effort. Conformation fortifies the creation of solid, healthy dogs that make excellent companions for generations to come. A champion show dog is considered to have superior genes. These exceptional specimens continue to "improve" the breed by producing puppies.

Even the most physically perfect example of a Pomeranian must be trained for the show ring beginning at a very early age.

A Pomeranian Puppy should be taught to tolerate grooming, posing, hands-on inspection, and exposure to noisy crowds as well as other dogs. They must present proper movement and temperament. Good nutrition is a key element for developing a successful show dog. Regular, appropriate exercise is required to build and maintain muscle. All of that criterion PLUS the cost and labor involved in grooming a top show coat – is a considerable commitment. Raising a successful show Pomeranian may be an expensive venture, but the experience of earning a title and working closely with your dog produces rewards that are life-long and PRICELESS!

Pomeranian Therapy Dog – Can this Breed be a Good Therapy Dog?

Volunteering your services and those of your dog in a therapy/comfort dog program is one of the most gratifying endeavors imaginable. Therapy dogs are trained to provide affection, comfort, and love to people confined to nursing homes, hospitals, rehabilitation centers, and hospice care. They visit schools, disaster areas, police stations, and other care facilities. Therapy dogs may provide emotional assistance to individuals suffering from conditions such as post-traumatic stress, autism, and various anxiety disorders. Therapy dogs are <u>NOT</u> service dogs. A therapy dog is naturally friendly, well-mannered, and has satisfied the basic training requirements for certification. Therapy dogs extend comfort and cheer through contact with patients and people in need. Their special brand of "therapy" is proven to relieve depression, diminish stress, reduce anxiety, and promote health.

A happy, cuddly, affectionate Pomeranian is an ideal candidate for a therapy dog program. The small, lightweight size is well suited for sick, institutionalized patients. An adorable Pom can comfortably perch on a wheelchair or cuddle in a bed with a child or older person. A Therapy Pomeranian must be calm, well-socialized, and indifferent to various and sudden sounds, ground surfaces, scents, equipment, and people. They must exhibit solid basic obedience training. A therapy dog should be at least one year of age, confirmed to be in good health by a qualified veterinarian, and in most cases registered with a certified therapy dog organization. Pomeranians retired from the show circuit make especially effective therapy dogs.

Pomeranian Service Dog – Can the Pomeranian be a Service Dog?

A Service Dog is a highly trained special assistant to a person with a disability such as; mobility limitations, visual impairment, hearing impairment, anxiety disorders, seizures, and diabetes. A special-assist Service Dog may train for years to provide the necessary assistance to their human partner. Dogs are selected and trained based on specific requirements, but all service dogs should demonstrate a solid temperament, exceptional trainability, and be in excellent health regardless of the vocation. Nearly any breed or mix of breeds can become a service dog, based on the human need. Special-assist Service Dogs are protected by the Americans with Disabilities Act (and similarly protected status in various countries) and are provided with access to all public areas designated by that law.

The most common Service Dogs are German Shepherds, Golden Retrievers, and Labrador Retrievers. Obviously, a Pomeranian cannot pull a wheelchair or navigate a busy street as a "seeing eye dog," but the little Poms' intelligence and aptitude for training make this breed a wonderful choice for certain individual disorders. Since a Pom can travel nearly anywhere with their human, people with anxiety disorders, epilepsy, diabetes, and severe allergies find the portable little Pomeranian the ideal special-assist Service Dog.

Is the Pomeranian the Best Breed for Your Family?

Selecting a Pomeranian as a pet goes beyond an appreciation of the breed's stunning appearance and charming personality. Understanding the traits of the breed prepares new owners for the lifelong commitment to housing, training, grooming, socialization, and health care. Complete due diligence also establishes an awareness of the dog's ability to acclimate and thrive within the family dynamics.

Do Pomeranian and Children get along?

Pomeranians are after all toy dogs. As such, they should make perfect pets for families with small children – right? That misconception has sent a number of Poms to rescue organizations, emergency veterinarian clinics, and sadly even resulted in death. The Pomeranian is a sturdy, robust dog with a reputation for being sassy. They may become over-protective, territorial, and if not properly socialized — downright nasty. Behavioral attributes aside, the Pom has a tiny, diminutive body with fragile bones that are easily broken. Injuries resulting from simply jumping off a piece of furniture, falling down stairs, or being dropped or stepped on, are common. Children must always be taught to approach, respect, and handle a Pom with care.

Young children should be supervised when playing with any pet.

A well-trained, child-friendly Pomeranian can be wonderful companion pet for children. They are small enough to be held, and the danger of the dog knocking even a small tot down is rare. A child can walk a Pom on a leash without being overpowered by the dog, and Pomeranians are not scary or intimidating to younger children.

Many breeders do not recommend a Pomeranian for families with children under 10 years of age. Poms can be intolerant of children's behavior. The noise of running and playing tends to upset, agitate or frighten the small dog. The breed's tendency to become territorial over toys, food, even family members can prove to be a problem in a family with children. The dog may react to perceived threats by growling, snapping, or biting. Children should be taught to always play with dogs in a gentle manner. Parents should supervise children and dogs to ensure appropriate behavior and to avoid unfortunate mishaps. Demonstrate to your child by your example, how to nurture and respect all dogs.

Pomeranians learn to coexist best with other animals if they are raised together.

Getting Along with other Pets – Pomeranian Dogs and Cats

Pomeranians are naturally curious, friendly animals. If properly socialized, in addition to their human family they enjoy the exposure to other people and animals.

Like other dogs, Pomeranians learn to coexist best with other pets, if they are raised together. Many Poms live harmoniously with different household pets like birds, rabbits, hamsters, and cats.

A dog-friendly cat and a Pom can bond and become great companions. If the cat is not accepting, it will most likely choose to stay away from the yappy, annoying dog. Regardless of the dynamics, supervision should be provided when introducing any new pet to the household.

Are Pomeranians Hypoallergenic – What if you suffer from Pet Allergies?

Pomeranians as a breed have an abundance of wonderful traits. They are a beautiful, animated teddy bear of a dog. Poms have a glorious, long, dense coat of glossy fur and they shed – a lot! That physical trait alone … rules out the idea of a Pomeranian being hypoallergenic.

It should be recognized that no dog is truly "hypoallergenic." Any animal can trigger an allergic reaction in individuals with sensitivities. In addition to the response to fur, people will develop allergy symptoms if exposed to dander, saliva, and parasites like fleas, that a dog can transmit. If you are a person with allergy sensitivities or suffer from respiratory issues like asthma, you may not be a good match for a Pomeranian.

Popular Pomeranian Puppy Names

What's in a name? A lot, if you are deciding on the best fit for your precious pet. Names are a big decision for pet owners. While there are no hard, fast rules, a name should represent your best effort for your puppy. Registry names can be long and impressive. Often, breeders will dictate a part of the registered name, so the breeding kennel is recognized. In those cases, the dog is given a short "call name" or nickname. The end result of any name should be fun, easy for the dog to understand (one or two syllables is recommended), and simple for you (and others) to remember and use.

Some popular names for Pomeranian Dogs include; Angel, Baby, Bella, Blacky, Buddy, Breezer, Candy, Coco, Dolly, Goldie, Red, Lola, Foxy, Teddy, and Snowy. A quick search of the Internet for "Pomeranian Names," will deliver addresses for several sites with an extensive list of names for both male and female Pomeranians.

CHAPTER 3

Pomeranian Puppies and Pomeranian Adult Dogs for Sale

The Pomeranian Dog is among the most popular breeds for companion pets. Many people admire and seek to own one or more of the classic, real-life teddy bears. The public demand, unfortunately, leads to over-breeding, poor breeding practices, backyard breeders looking to make a quick profit, and commercial breeding facilities (also known as puppy mills). Irresponsible and unknowledgeable breeding practices can lead to frail health issues and genetically bad temperaments and seriously damage the breed as a whole. Before adopting the dog of your dreams, an important consideration should be given to gender, age, price, and where to find your Pomeranian.

Pomeranian Puppies for Sale – Where to look for a Good Quality Pomeranian Puppy

Adopting a Pomeranian is a family affair. Do you prefer a male or a female dog? Should your new pet be a young puppy or a mature dog? The expectations of each family member should be considered as well as who is going to share the responsibility of care and training. Perhaps the most important of all the decisions regarding the addition of a dog is the source for obtaining the family pet. There are dozens of choices, how do you make the right buying decision?

An appropriate place to begin your search for a great Pomeranian breeder is the dog show circuit. The AKC and other breeder clubs post announcements about local, state, and national conformation shows. The shows are open to the public. Dog shows provide the opportunity to compare breeds as well as the study difference in dogs within a breed. Most shows feature a "Meet and Greet" exhibit. Interested spectators can handle the dogs and talk with breeders, handlers, and groomers about the breed. Dog shows also sell specialty catalogs with the names and contact information of member breeders.

National dog magazines, fancy online ads, and local newspaper advertisements do not certify a reputable source for your puppy. Anyone can buy advertising space. It is the responsibility of the buyer to do the homework to determine a good breeder.

When you find breeders of interest, plan to visit the kennels where their puppies are being nurtured. A good breeder will NOT sell a dog to someone they haven't met in person. They will encourage prospective buyers to spend time with the puppies and interact with the litter. Make multiple visits if desired. Before committing to buy, it should be expected you will ask for the breeder's client references and check them.

A good breeder cares deeply about their breeding program, but more importantly, they care about the dogs they produce. They will encourage visits to their kennel and invite the entire family. As a prospective buyer, you should expect to complete a purchase application and provide references. The breeder will be interested in why you will make a good pet parent for one of their precious babies. You may anticipate questions such as

- Why do you want a Pomeranian Puppy?
- How much time will you have for the care of the puppy?
- Do you have other pets?
- Do you have small children?
- Do you have a fenced yard?
- Can you provide adequate exercise, mental stimulation, and socialization?
- What are your training plans?
- Are you prepared to provide adequate grooming?

Do not be alarmed if the breeder does not choose to sell a Pomeranian Puppy to you immediately. In fact, many breeders will reserve making a decision and will even put prospective buyers on a "wait list." They do not sell to the first person with cash in hand. They want to find the right home for their dog, and the decision is often a gut instinct. It may take a certain commitment from a buyer to demonstrate persistence, to make the good impression stick.

Buying a Pomeranian – What are the Warning Signs to Avoid?

Locating a safe, reliable source for your Pomeranian Dog is of the utmost importance. A solid, healthy dog offers a lifetime of comfort and happiness. A dog suffering from health problems can be a devastating heartache. There is an abundance of Pomeranians advertised for sale in newspapers, magazines, and on the Internet. They are offered by responsible breeders, dog farmers, dog brokers, and various rescue groups. Poms can be found at rescue shelters, dog pounds, pet stores, flea markets, and from the trunks of cars in parking lots. The choices can be overwhelming and make for an impulsive buy. Choosing your Pom based on price and convenience is a temptation. There are warning signs of what to avoid if you expect to purchase a quality pet.

Before you buy any dog, visit the breeding location and look for red flags such as

- The mother of the litter is not on the premises
- Dogs are held in cramped, dirty kennels
- Several dogs of various breeds are on the grounds
- Multiple litters are enclosed with several nursing females
- Multiple pregnant females
- Dogs around the property are restrained on chains
- Multiple dogs are held together in pens
- Dogs on the premise are dirty, appear malnourished, or sick
- Females can deliver a litter every 6 months

- The "breeder" is willing to let a puppy go too young (less than 8 weeks of age)
- Prices that are too low or too expensive

Do not buy a Pomeranian if you do not meet the parents – at the very least see the mother and visit the location of the litter's birth. Do not fall for the clean, cute, corral inside a house with no other visible dogs on the premise. Brokers will often purchase a litter from a puppy mill and sell to unsuspecting buyers as "home bred dogs."

Beware of a Pomeranian that costs too little – or too much!

Pomeranian Puppies Price – How much is that Doggie in the Window?

Pomeranian Puppies are offered in a wide range of prices. Depending on where the puppy is purchased and the pedigree of the dog the price may be as low as $300 (243.54 EUR) or as much as $5,000 (4059 EUR). Typically, a buyer may anticipate paying between $600 (487.08 EUR) and $2,000 (1623.60 EUR) for a Pom Puppy. Remember, if a price is too low to be true, or too high to be believable, it represents a big red warning flag.

The expense of a Pomeranian Puppy doesn't stop with the purchase price. Annual fees for health care, nutrition, training, grooming, registrations, and other 'essentials' should be budgeted. Experts recommend allocating approximately $1,000 (1623.60 EUR) annually to provide proper basic care for a pet quality Pomeranian Dog.

Adult Pomeranian Price – What should you expect to pay?

Deciding if you are up to the training and development needs of a young puppy versus the stability and maturity of an adult dog is the first step. Another factor in choosing between a young pup versus an older dog may involve cost. Adult dogs are often surrendered to shelters by owners unable to continue their care, and they make good pets. Often, breeders will sell Poms retired from their breeding program at a fair price. Pomeranians that are two years old or older are often available for adoption fees of a few hundred dollars.

Pomeranian Price Range – Why the Wide Range of Prices?

The purchase price of a Pomeranian ranges from a few hundred dollars to a several thousand. There are no government regulations to monitor the fees associated with buying a dog. Various factors contribute to the price tag. Determining a fair, reasonable price for a sound, healthy Pomeranian is entirely left to what the buyer is willing to pay.

Elements of the basic fees involve the individual Pomeranian selected. The litter order (do you want the "pick of the litter"), standard, conformation, pedigree, championship bloodlines, color, and markings are among the components that determine the selling price.

What's on paper? The type of registration of the dog is a variable in considering the fee. If you plan to show or breed your dog, the registration is considerably more expensive. If your interest is in obtaining a sound, pet quality Pom, the registration is "limited" meaning you cannot show or breed. Many breeders require proof of spaying or neutering a Pomeranian sold with a limited registration agreement.

Time is money. The age of the dog will also have a bearing on the price. The optimal window for breeders to sell a litter is six weeks (litter pick with deposit). Puppies may transition to their forever homes at 8-weeks to 10-weeks of age. Puppies that are not sold by the time they are 3 months old are reduced in price. It is pure supply/demand economics and no reflection of the quality of the Pom. Most buyers desire to acquire a puppy during their first formative stages of development. They fail to appreciate the advantages of older dogs so as the puppy ages, the demand decreases and so does the price.

Location, location, location! The price of Pomeranian Dogs and Pomeranian Puppies varies, depending on where you live. State laws and ordinances restrict breeding practices in certain areas.

There are licenses, taxes and other fees associated with breeding and selling a dog, that will impact the cost to the buyer. States with fewer restrictions will often become a haven for puppy mills and the irresponsible breeders who churn out puppies for profit resulting in the gross overpopulation of Pomeranians, as well as other dogs. In these states, prices may be considerably less than in stricter regulated areas. The weather is also a factor in the location of purchase. Breeders in northern regions with inclement winters will often sell puppies at a lower price during the cold season.

The color of money. It may be assumed, a Pomeranian's color means everything when it comes to cost. Pomeranians produce the widest array of colors of any purebred breed. Orange Poms are the most common and consequently the least expensive. Rare, pure black, and pure white, and exotic colors like lavender, or blue, and certain coat color combinations will increase the cost. Generally, the rarer the color, the more expensive the Pomeranian.

Teacup Pomeranian Puppies for Sale – Where to find a Teacup Pomeranian

Advertisement for selling *"Teacup Pomeranians,"* or *"Toy Pomeranians,"* and *"Miniature Pomeranians"* should be considered something of a scam. The Pomeranian is a small dog classified in the Toy Group among kennel clubs. The breed standard defines the weight of an ideal adult Pomeranian Dog as 3 to 7 lbs. (1.36 to 3.175 kgs.). Deliberately producing, advertising, and promoting dogs that are below (or above) the breed standard is not only irresponsible, but the very practice contributes to serious health issues within the breed.

Perro Pomeranian for Sale – What, Where, and how much is a Perro Pomeranian?

There is much to be said for a name. *"Perro Pomeranian,"* sounds rare, exotic, elusive and oh so romantic. It makes the prospective buyer want to dig for a wallet and grab the opportunity to own an authentic Perro Pom! Almost! The name *Perro* is actually the Spanish translation of the word *Dog*. So, purchasing a Perro Pomeranian Dog or a Perro Pomeranian Puppy from any source is simply buying a *Pomeranian Dog!*

CHAPTER 4

Pomeranian Breeding – What are the Best Breeding Practices?

How can a breed like the Pomeranian remain so consistent when predicting the size, weight, appearance, overall health, and even the temperament of the adult dog? The dependable result is thanks to some hundred plus years of sincere efforts by devoted breeders. Responsible breeders strive to create the best possible formula to produce quality, exceptional puppies that may become world champion competitors or perfect pets. They learn from each litter and from canine educators, medical experts, and other breeders. A "Best Breeding Practices" guide is considered the "Bible" for a responsible breeder.

A good breeder does not produce puppies for profit. In fact, the cost of breeding a quality litter is barely a break-even proposition. Researching pedigrees, visiting kennels and sourcing a good, solid bitch (mother) and stud (father) is just the beginning of the *cha-ching* investment.

Pomeranians are known as the "heartbreak breed."

Pomeranian Breeders – What are the Signs of a Responsible Pomeranian Breeder?

It isn't difficult to spot a human in love with their Pomeranian. When that love extends to create a passionate Pomeranian breeder, you are in luck! The person that cares about their puppies' well-being and treats their breeding stock like family will do everything possible to produce good babies.

Some indications of a good, responsible breeder are easy to verify. A concerned breeder follows breeding best practices including the selection of breeding pairs, health testing, the frequency of breeding, the whelping and rearing of puppies, socialization, and placement of the babies.

Quality breeders care deeply about their breeding program, but more importantly, they care about the dogs they produce. They will encourage visits to their kennel and invite the entire family. As a prospective buyer, you should expect to complete a puppy purchase application and provide references. The breeder will be interested in why you will make a good pet parent for one of their precious babies. You may anticipate questions such as

- Why do you want a Pomeranian Puppy?
- How much time will you have for the care of the puppy?
- Do you have other pets?
- Do you have small children?
- Do you have a fenced yard?
- Can you provide adequate exercise, mental stimulation, and socialization?
- What are your training plans?
- Are you prepared to provide adequate grooming?

There are obvious signs to look for to confirm a reputable breeding practice.

1. **A hygienic living environment.** A safe, clean kennel with fresh water and toys is essential to raising healthy puppies.
2. **The puppies are inside the home.** Pomeranian pups destined to become pets should be raised inside the house, not in the garage, barn, yard, or basement.
3. **The breeder doesn't advertise exotic, nonstandard Pomeranian specialties** ("Teacup Pomeranians," or rare colors).
4. **The breeder participates in dog shows.** Breeding dogs that are confirmed examples of the breed standard is demonstrated by show championships.

5. **The breeder requires a puppy purchase agreement** that includes a return policy and a spay/neuter contract.

6. **A good breeder provides a full and honest disclosure** about the breed in general and the specific puppy of interest.

7. **A concerned breeder wants to meet your family.**

8. **The responsible breeder provides a puppy care package** that includes a minimum of: health certificates, a full pedigree for both parents, care instructions, starter food.

9. **A responsible breeder is available** for questions, concerns, advice, and assistance to buyers.

10. **A good breeder remains committed to their dogs for life.**

Breeding Pomeranian Dogs – How to Start a Pomeranian Breeding Program

In the genes – Quality Pomeranians with great bloodlines are expected to transfer their prodigious genes to their offspring. Experienced, responsible breeders recognize a puppy is only as good as the dogs it comes from. Breeders with the mission to produce exemplary dogs start with the selection of the mating pair.

Pomeranian breeders are active members of their breed clubs providing an affiliation with respected breeders around the world. The network supports breeding programs with an excellent source of information and education. It also establishes a foundation for procuring potential breeding stock. Breeders share information about successful breeding results as well as disappointing ventures. They populate an extensive database that tracks health conditions and pedigrees.

Breeding Pomeranian Dogs – How to Select a Pomeranian for Breeding?

Any Pomeranian entering a breeding program should be a show quality puppy from a bloodline of proven conformation champions. The budget for a quality breeding female Pomeranian will run between $1000 (811.80 EUR) and $5000 (4059 EUR), or more. The price of the male will depend on if the dog is purchased by the breeder, or if the breeder chooses to use the dog as a stud. Fees for males may range from $500 (405.90 EUR) for stud service to several thousand dollars to purchase a proven, champion stud dog.

Best Breeding Practices require any Pomeranian Dog considered for a breeding program clear a strict health testing protocol. DNA panels look for a variety of genetic conditions. These tests are critical to prevent passing a congenital disease like epilepsy, some cancers, and undesirable physical traits. Intense medical exams by qualified animal healthcare professionals are also mandated. Eye evaluations (CERFs) are performed to identify eye disease, a cardiac exam looks for heart murmurs and establishes good heart health. A radiologist uses x-rays to detect orthopedic issues like hip dysplasia, patellar luxation, and open fontanels. A BAER test is conducted to eliminate concerns of deafness and disorders of the ears. Failure to pass any of the tests should result in the breeder removing the Pomeranian from the breeding program. A responsible breeder will provide confirmation of these tests with results, along with the puppy health certifications, for any Pom they sell.

Breeding Pomeranian Dogs – How to Prepare a Pomeranian for Breeding

The Pomeranian Best Breeding Practices recognizes the importance of quality nutrition in the physical and mental development of dogs in a breeding program. Dogs should receive regular health examinations and be free of any parasites or communicable diseases like Bordetella (kennel cough), parvovirus, distemper, brucellosis, and rabies. Breeding Pomeranian must be well-groomed, exercised, and socialized. A clean, safe, housing environment is required for the dog's overall well-being and the puppies' good health.

It is strongly suggested that any breeding Pomeranian be "finished" by a sanctioned kennel club. In doing so, the breeder offers the buyer the assurance the mating pair is indeed a great representation of the breed.

Mating dogs should be fully physically mature – at least one year of age. A female Pomeranian should not give birth to more than one litter a year – regardless of the size of the litter. Some kennel clubs, including the AKC, limit the number of litter registrations they will accept from one female. A female Pomeranian should be retired from breeding by 7 years of age. Inbreeding (father/daughter, mother/son, and full siblings) is discouraged. It is recommended puppies remain with their mother for at least 8 weeks during which time they must be kept clean, well-fed, and provided with qualified medical care at regular intervals for health checks, vaccinations, and worming. The litter should be registered with a sanctioned kennel club.

Breeding Pomeranian Dogs – Types of Pomeranian Breeding

Female Pomeranians experience a "season," or "heat" cycle, twice a year beginning around 6 months of age. A female Pom should not be bred until she is fully developed, physically mature, and able to carry, deliver and care for a healthy litter of puppies. Only during a short period of time in her heat cycle will a female will accept the male dog and become pregnant. Intact male dogs (unneutered), on the other hand, will breed with any receptive female dog —ANYTIME! A male dog should also be physically mature before he is allowed to breed.

Natural Breeding — When a female Pomeranian and a male Pom mate it is referred to as a natural or "live breeding." Natural breeding is the most common way to impregnate a female Pom. Natural breeding requires that both the female and male are physically present at the time the female is willing to mate. Most breeders enclose the breeding pair together several times over the course of the female's viable days to ensure optimal results from the mating.

Artificial Insemination — Technology offers another option for breeding. Artificial insemination (AI) has become increasingly popular among breeders. AI begins with the collection of sperm from the male Pomeranian. The sperm is either used within 24 hours of the collection or deposited in a vial, frozen, and stored appropriately. When the female Pomeranian is determined ready to impregnate, the sperm is thawed and immediately injected into the female. Frozen sperm may be used years after collection. Most kennel clubs, including the AKC, offer registration for purebred dogs conceived by either method.

Mis-Mating — Dogs have no discrimination when it comes to the innate desire to procreate. A female in heat will go to extreme measures to breed, and nothing in nature is wilier and determined than the intact male dog's drive to mate with a viable female dog. It is extremely important to recognize heat cycles and keep dogs separated when mating is not the optimum outcome. Copulation happens very quickly. Dogs can tunnel under floors, jump barriers, sneak into houses; they can even mate through fences. The result of mismating is an "oops litter." Oops litters can produce puppies from mothers/sons, fathers/daughters, and siblings. They can also produce offspring from completely different breeds. In fact, a female in heat left unattended may give birth to puppies from different male dogs in the same litter. Unfortunately, many pups produced by an accidental mating end up in shelters. It is vitally important for owners to spay or neuter their pet to protect against unwanted pregnancy and ultimately the "oops" puppies resulting from these encounters.

Copulation happens very quickly. Determined
dogs can even breed through fences!

Breeding Pomeranian Dogs – How to Care for a New Born Litter of Pomeranian Puppies

In most cases, a female Pomeranian, like other female animals, has the necessary instinct to care for her newborn babies properly. Except in unusual circumstances, the birthing process should be left to the mother. Given a safe whelping bed she will deliver the babies, bite through the umbilical cords, tear the amniotic sacs, clean the newborn, and nudge them to nurse.

For the first few weeks of life, the mother Pom will assume the responsibility for the care of her offspring. The mother's milk provides for all of the nutritional needs of the young. It also delivers immunities for the first 4 to 6 weeks of life. The puppies will nurse every two hours for the first four weeks of life. As the puppies grow and demand more food, it becomes increasingly difficult for the mother Pom to produce enough milk to satisfy their growing bodies. It is time to transition to puppies to solid food. At about five weeks of age the mother dog will slowly stop nursing the puppies, and at six to seven weeks of age, she will have them weaned from nursing completely.

A healthy newborn Pomeranian will weigh about two ounces. They should gain 10% to 15% of their birth weight a day. Newborns should regularly be weighed, and their growth charted, to ensure they are gaining weight and thriving.

It is essential to keep the whelping bed clean, warm, and to make fresh drinking water constantly available for the Pomeranian mother. Her diet will change, and she will require additional food to produce enough milk for her puppies. As the puppies become more mobile, they will need expanding space to exercise, explore, and play. It is necessary that the playpen for the puppies is clean, and a constant supply of fresh drinking water is available to them.

Pomeranians are known as the "heartbreak breed." Female Poms have small litters, and the newborns frequently die. A newborn that weighs one ounce or less will usually die shortly after birth. Bigger litters are especially susceptible to low birth weights. Puppies that survive the birthing experience beyond the first 48 hours typically live long, healthy, natural lives.

Where to find Specialty Pomeranian Breeders

Pomeranian Dogs come in the widest variety of colors, patterns, and markings of any purebred breed. The American Kennel Club recognizes 18 different colors and 9 definitions of markings in the breed standard. Pomeranians are the result of years of selective breeding practices by dedicated, skilled breeders. Evolving from dogs of the Nordic regions, the Pomeranian eventually developed from the 20 to 30-pound Spitz, to the diminutive Pom we know and love today.

Of the many colors of this lovely breed, there are some coats considered rarer and more "exotic" than other coats. Most of the rare colors are simply the result of the presence of a dominant gene. In some cases, rare colors are also associated with serious health risks like blindness and deafness. It is recommended that potential owners carefully research colors and markings to ensure they are buying a Pomeranian Puppy that is both recognized by kennel club registries, and free from congenital defects.

There are serious, experienced breeders who are committed to studying the genetic science of a Pomeranian's coloring, among other characteristics. Such experts may be able to breed and predict a puppy's adult coat reliably. However, advertisements for "Irish Marked Pomeranian Breeders," and "Brindle Pomeranian Breeders," or "Exotic Pomeranian Breeders," should be considered with skepticism. Ads offering "Merle Pomeranian Breeders," and "Teacup Pomeranian Breeders" or other abnormal, "rare" Poms, should be avoided. Breeding practices designed to produce dogs outside the established breed standard are not ethical.

People often surrender their Poms for rehoming. There are any variety of reasons for giving a dog up. A responsible, compassionate breeder is a part of their puppies' lives forever and will make arrangements to take a Pomeranian back to rehome, if necessary.

CHAPTER 5

Pomeranian Dog Adoption – What are the Crucial Things to Consider?

You have researched the Pomeranian Dog breed and decided to give a rescue Pom a good forever home is the right path to follow. If adoption is the right choice, you have several options available. Pomeranians are among the most popular purebred breeds in the world. As such, many are produced annually and sadly, many Pomeranians find themselves at the mercy of rescue shelters. People surrender their Poms to shelters for a variety of reasons.

Pomeranian Dog Rescue – What Happened to these Dogs?

Estimates indicate some 25% of dogs in shelters are purebreds.

People surrender their Poms to shelters for a variety of reasons. Divorce, relocation, illness, death, allergies, loss of income, or simply they are not able to deal with the demands of owning a Pomeranian.

Dogs in rehoming situations are typically 3 to 7 years of age. Some breed-specific rescue groups will take a dog if he or she not a purebred but has some Pomeranian physical traits. Most rehomed dogs bond quickly with new families and reward the kindness with gratitude and love.

Pomeranian Dog Rescue Organizations – Where to Look for Rescues

There are several options for locating an available Pomeranian for adoption. Breeders are a good source of information. Responsible breeders require an agreement from buyers stating they will return a dog, should they no longer be able to keep their Pom. Breeders also regularly retire dogs from their breeding program, and from show competitions. Such dogs may be offered for rehoming. These Pomeranian are usually well-socialized, healthy, solid dogs with varying degrees of training, and looking forward to a forever retirement home.

Pomeranian kennel clubs are another good resource for locating adoptable dogs. Most clubs support a breed rescue committee. These groups provide temporary foster homes for Pomeranians surrendered to shelters, or otherwise abandoned. In foster care, the Poms are fully vetted, and their temperaments are tested. If necessary, they are housetrained and socialized. Identified issues regarding health, temperament, or behavior, are disclosed to prospective adoptive parents.

Rescue shelters, community pounds, the Humane Society, and veterinarian offices are all good organizations to investigate in search of an adoptable Pomeranian.

Pomeranians fostered at rescue groups are medically evaluated. In most cases dogs are fully vaccinated, spayed or neutered, and treated for health conditions before they are released to rehome. Pomeranians with serious problems like biting are deemed not eligible for adoption.

Pomeranian Dog for Adoption near me?

Most local rescue groups are very visible in the community and easy to find. Advertisements in local newspapers and occasionally on television keep interested patrons informed of available dogs for adoption. Communities also support a humane society or "dog pound" and their animal control efforts. To find a local rescue, check with veterinarian offices, groomers, and area law enforcement's animal control division. Online sites like Pet Finder (www.petfinder.com) maintain a database of pets available for adoption with pictures, videos, and a sort range by breed, age, and postal / zip code.

Pomeranian Puppy Rescue – How to Care for a Rescued Puppy

Pomeranian puppy rescues are usually 7 months of age or older. Occasionally law enforcement officers will be called in to close an illegal commercial breeding facility/puppy mill, and the dogs on the premises are confiscated and sent to shelters for care and rehoming. Nursing puppies are kept with their mothers whenever possible. As soon as the dogs are rehabilitated, they are offered for adoption. Rescued Pomeranians of any age should be cared for just like a puppy carefully selected and purchased from a breeder. They require quality, breed appropriate food, training, socialization, and medical care. If the puppy is old enough, they are spayed or neutered before rehoming. Special health conditions may require extra medical care. In such cases, the new human parents should be notified, and care instructions provided.

Pomeranian Dog Rescue – How can you help?

The Humane Society of the United States reports some 25 percent of dogs in animal shelters are purebreds. Want to help? The very interest demonstrated in a rescue group or shelter is of assistance to the animals confined. Human time, money, attention, and other efforts go a long, long way. Volunteer! There are any number of jobs available at shelters. Donate supplies like food, bowls, toys, blankets, rugs, bleach, and detergents. If you don't have the physical means to help, share information. Repost photos of available dogs and cats. There are no "little jobs" in animal rescue. Do what you can to help secure a forever home for the many dogs in need.

CHAPTER 6

Pomeranian Supplies – What do you Need?

After searching for the perfect Pomeranian, you finally selected the right dog for your family and the big day is near. Time to bring the baby home! Preparing the house for the arrival is no easy task. Tiny Pomeranian puppies are very adept at getting in big trouble surprisingly fast. They will chew on electrical cords, plants, walls, and eat anything they can *almost* manage to swallow. They can fall down stairs, get stuck under appliances, wedge behind furniture, and create an entire world of danger and destruction in their new surroundings. Puppy proofing the home is essential, for everyone's safety and security.

A nutritious diet is crucial to your Pomeranian's well-being.

Pomeranian Dog Food – Best Food for Pomeranians

Good nutrition is critical for a healthy, well-adjusted dog for life. A Pomeranian puppy needs a special diet designed to meet the demands of a growing body. The Pomeranian adult requires a different diet to maintain optimal health. The Pomeranian senior dog may develop special needs. Your Pom's diet should be monitored to ensure the best program, for dog's stage of life.

Your breeder should send a puppy home with a few days' supply of food, and instructions for feeding. Note: any changes in food should be made gradually, to avoid digestive distress, regardless of the dog's age.

Small Breed Food – What are the Best Types for Pomeranians?

Blends developed by commercial dog food manufacturers are typically marketed based on the size of the adult dog (small, medium, large) rather than being breed-specific. A small breed food recommends different feeding guidelines and smaller nuggets, than food designed for larger dogs. Commercial dog food is packaged as dry kibble, wet (canned) food, freeze-dried food, frozen food, and raw food. Some pet owners prefer to prepare their Poms food at home. Recipes featuring ingredients for optimal health should be researched and followed for wholesome, homemade meals.

Commercial foods are monitored by government agencies. The ingredients used for production must be included on the packaging. Ingredients used for production are itemized by the content of the food. A premium quality dog food features:

- All-natural ingredients
- Wholesome real meat (listed first on the contents list)
- Wholesome real fruits and vegetables
- Includes fiber, healthy fats, and nutritional supplements
- Contains NO animal by-products or generic meat
- Contains NO fillers
- Contains NO harmful coloring or chemical preservatives
- Manufactured in the USA, Canada, or countries monitored by production safety guidelines

Pomeranian Puppy Food

The selection of puppy food available at retail can be overwhelming. Until a Pomeranian Puppy reaches one year of age, his or her body structure is continually forming. A home prepared diet may be ideal for an adult Pomeranian Dog, but the Pom Puppy requires a different ratio of nutrients like proteins, calcium, phosphorus, and even calories. It may be best to feed a top quality, commercially prepared food designed for "small breed puppies" to ensure your Pomeranian is getting the ideal diet during the critical, first-year growth periods.

Pomeranian Foods to Avoid

Pomeranian Dogs become so much a part of the family it may be difficult to avoid feeding "bad people food" to the fur-child. There are human foods that may cause an upset tummy, promote allergies, contribute to obesity and gastrointestinal disorders, and there are people foods that can be toxic, even fatal to a Pomeranian. Foods to avoid include

- Cooked bones
- Alcoholic beverages or foods prepared with alcohol
- Caffeine; coffee, tea, sodas
- Grapes and raisins
- Onions
- Nuts
- Artificial sweeteners
- Chocolate
- Fatty, greasy foods
- Table scraps

Pomeranians are notoriously picky eaters. In addition to compromising your Pom's health, the introduction of "people food" can seriously affect his eating habits. It can also promote the nuisance of "table begging." To maintain your Pomeranian's peak appearance, table manners, and good health – plan his or her diet and stick to it.

Pomeranian Dog Beds – Dog Beds that Provide the Best Comfort for Your Pomeranian

The right bed for your Pomeranian depends a good deal on the age and health of the individual dog. Beds are typically not a one-size-fits-all proposition. The right size bed for a Pom should satisfy the dog's need for comfort as well as safety and security. The bed should represent a nest for snuggling and relaxing. The little, dog should feel protected and warm to promote sound sleep.

Second to safety, a Pomeranian's bed must provide adequate support. The mattress should curve to the body's form and support the skeleton. The lack of proper support will lead to stiff, sore joints and a thinning coat.

A superior cover material is a critical component in a good bed. The luxurious coat of the Pom is the crowning glory. Contact friction can negatively affect the condition of the Pomeranian's coat. Contact friction occurs when the coat comes in contact with harsh, rough surfaces. The texture of the Pom's bed cover should be soft and gentle to the dog's coat.

No matter the dog's age or state of health, the Pomeranian's bed covering should be washable for easy laundering. Most experts recommend washing a dog's bed at least once a month, to maintain good hygiene.

Specialty beds featuring orthopedic mattresses, premium filling and covers, high bumpers, and raised beds are among the many designs available for your Pomeranian's style, comfort, and health considerations.

Pomeranian Dog Collar – How to Select a Pomeranian Collar that Perfectly Fits

From plain to bling, Pomeranian dog collars are available in every style to suit the dogs and the owner. Collars are more than a fashion statement. They serve many important purposes. A collar provides for the dog's safety when walking on a leash. They are a source for identification tags including owner contact information. A proper collar should be the right fit for the dog.

Collars are available in a variety of sizes. Most Pomeranian Adult Dogs will wear an extra small, 1" wide collar. To measure the dog's neck to ensure the correct size use a measuring tape, circle the neck securely where the collar will rest. Insert two fingers between the tape and the Pom's neck which will add approximately 2 inches to the length. Remember to check the fit frequently. The amount of fur between the neck and collar changes and will affect the fit as well as contributing to tangles and matting of the coat under the collar.

Pomeranians have especially fragile necks. As a breed, they often suffer from degenerative weakness of the tracheal rings (windpipe). Never use your Pomeranian's collar for lifting, holding, or pulling the dog. To reduce the risk of neck injuries harnesses are recommended for this breed.

Specialty behavior management collars such as Pomeranian bark collars and Pomeranian shock collars are too heavy. They are designed to distribute a sonic shock when activated by a remote. Such collars are not recommended as effective training tools for this toy breed and may cause serious health problems.

Pomeranian Dog Harness – When Should You Use a Harness?

The Pomeranian's vulnerable neck and the risk of injuries make a harness preferred in addition to or in place of a collar. Harnesses fit along the dog's shoulders, back, and chest. The tension from a leash is distributed along the sturdiest parts of the Pom's body and avoid the fragile neck area completely. Harnesses are most effective when training a Pomeranian to walk properly on lead. They minimize the dog's tendency to pull and provide for better handling. A harness is also an essential constraint for a Pom's safety when riding in a vehicle.

Harnesses come in three basic styles. Strap harnesses are a series of belts that cross around the dog's back, chest and shoulders. Strap harnesses are preferred for many breeds but may not be small enough for a Pomeranian. Wrap harnesses are small vests with a D-ring attached between the shoulder blades as a leash hook. Clothing harnesses are a type of jacket with a D-ring sewn in the back for a leash. The clothing harness is used when the Pomeranian needs extra protection from the weather. In addition to the type of harness you choose for your Pomeranian Dog, attention should be given to the size, material, and ease of getting the harness on and off the Pomeranian.

The Pomeranians big personality and insatiable curiosity make it critical to maintain control at all times when outdoors.

Pomeranian Dog Leash – What is the Ideal Type and Length of Leash?

Your Pomeranian's comfort and safety are of primary concerns in all matters – especially in the outdoor world. For a small dog with a big, big personality and insatiable curiosity, it is critical to maintain control at all times when your Pom is outdoors. With the decision of a proper harness and collar made the next step is to purchase an appropriate leash.

Leashes are available in a wide selection and are designed for function and style. They come in different lengths, material, and in both retractable and fixed lengths. Obviously, a 3-inch-wide, heavy corded leash, is too large for a Pomeranian. A nylon cord leash is suitable for small dogs. It is good to start training with a shorter leash for control. Short leashes are between 4 and 6 feet long. Depending on the area of exercise, your Pomeranian's training success, and the amount of stimuli, you may consider moving up to a retractable leash. Retractable leashes come in lengths from 10 feet to 50 feet, or more. They offer more freedom for the dog to run and are good tools for beginning agility training.

Pomeranian Dog Muzzle – How to Find a Muzzle that Fits Your Pomeranian

The idea of using a muzzle on a tiny dog like a Pomeranian seems a bit excessive. After all, a muzzle is for big, dangerous dogs – right? Actually, muzzles may be used for the safety of the dog, a person, or both. If injured and in need of emergency care, it may be necessary to muzzle the animal. The use of dog muzzles, especially for a Pomeranian may be controversial, but when necessary it is essential the right size and style of muzzle be used.

A dog in pain or a frightened dog has the tendency to bite. Injured dogs and dogs in need of emergency care, may be necessary to muzzle. The groomer or veterinarian's office could request a muzzle to prevent an accident if a dog experiences heightened anxiety. Some agencies also require therapy dogs be muzzled when working, especially if exposed to children.

Basket muzzles are designed to prevent biting. They look a bit intimidating, but they are considered the safest and most humane muzzle available. A basket muzzle fits over the dog's mouth and extends up his nose, with enough room for the animal to breathe easily and drink water. Basket muzzles are made from wire mesh, plastic mesh, or pliable plastic. The plastic models are recommended for small dogs. The smallest basket muzzle is appropriate for a Pomeranian Dog.

Soft muzzles are made from rope, mesh, or leather. Soft muzzles are not as comfortable as a basket model. The straps fit around the dog's head and circles his muzzle, preventing the opening of the jaws.

Manufacturers advertise muzzles for a variety of behavioral modifications, in addition to controlling biting including reducing barking and chewing. Such methods are not recommended, as no muzzle should be used for an extended period of time, or without supervision.

Pomeranian Dog Crates – What is the Best Size Crate?

The use of a crate can prove priceless, as your Pomeranian transitions to its new home. Crates preserve the safety and security of the dog, and the owner. A crate for a Pomeranian should be large enough for the adult dog to stand and turn around. Crate dividers may be used if the adult size crate is too large. Crates are sold in various models. They are constructed of wire, plastic, and soft-sided materials. The crate you choose should be chew resistant, and any opening like vents should be small enough to prevent your Pom from getting caught between wires or in holes. Soft-sided crates should not have exposed zippers or attachments that may be chewed off and swallowed. Latches should be secured to prevent escape.

Pomeranian Travel Crate

The portability of a Pomeranian is one of the breed's most desired traits. While a regular crate for this little dog is small enough to be transported in planes, trains, and automobiles there are other alternatives when traveling. Carriers for Pomeranian Dogs come in many styles. There are soft-sided shoulder carriers, vented backpacks, pull crates with wheels, and large doggie totes.

Pomeranian Trailers – What is the Best Size Trailer for Pomeranians?

Pomeranian trailers are used to transport a Pom or other small dogs behind a bicycle, or as a buggy stroller with his human. It is a means to take your precious pup along when walking is too long, or strenuous. A comfortable trailer suitable for a Pomeranian should be equipped with a safe, escape-proof compartment, a mesh screen for proper ventilation, a seatbelt, and wheel brakes.

Pomeranian Dog Kennel – What is the Best Size Kennel for Pomeranians?

A Pomeranian is a small, companion dog that should be kept indoors unless constantly supervised. Indoor/outdoor exercise kennels or playpens are available in several different sizes. A small, 35 square inch enclosure with 26-inch tall panels is ideal for a little dog like the Pomeranian. Made of plastic, wire, or mesh, these versatile kennels are wonderful to keep your Pomeranian in a secure, confined space for training or rest. The open slats allow your Pom to see you and other activities in the room. The convertible, expandable panels of most kennels make moving to different areas of the house and yard a simple task.

Pomeranian Dog House – How Big Should They Be, and Which Features Should They Include?

A Pomeranian Dog is an indoor pet. The diminutive size and fragile nature of the breed make their survival outdoors nearly impossible. Indoor housing provisions must be made if adding a Pomeranian to your family is a consideration.

The aspect of an indoor dog does not eliminate the idea of a Pomeranian Dog House. For fun or functionality, a comfortable, cute house may be created using cardboard, craft wood, plastic slats, or even quilted cloth. A Pomeranian Dog House must be big enough for the dog to stand, turn around, and lay down. The door should allow for easy entry and exit. Make sure there are no ornaments the dog can break off, chew and swallow. A crate pad, blankets, or a warm rug will make for a nice den of comfort for your pampered Pom.

*Designing a functional, safe, indoor dog house
for your Pomeranian is a fun project.*

Pomeranian Dog Grooming Supplies – What Grooming Products Provide the Best Results for Your Pomeranian?

The Pomeranian Dog's magnificent coat is truly its most distinguishing physical feature. Long, dense, glossy, glorious fur is the best representative of a healthy, cared-for dog. Good Pomeranian grooming doesn't end with the coat. The conscientious owner commits to caring for the whole dog. The best results are directly related to the tools.

The proper bathing schedule for your Pomeranian depends on the dog's health, activity, and the living environment. Bathing too frequently can dry the skin and coat. Too few baths may allow dirt, oil, and grim to build making the coat mat, tangle, and lose its natural luster.

What is the Best Shampoo and Condition for your Pomeranian?

There is a vast selection of pet shampoos and conditioners available at retail sites. Most promise "superior results" and the hype can be very convincing and confusing. It is important to select products designed for the specific coat of your Pomeranian. NEVER use human products on your dog. All grooming products should be of an appropriate size for a small dog like the Pomeranian.

Good shampoos for Pomeranians should be gentle and pH balanced for canines. Quality products nourish the skin and fur with natural ingredients like aloe, eucalyptus, almond oil, green tea, and oatmeal. Shampoos and conditioners containing synthetic dyes, perfumes, parabens, and phosphates can dry the skin, and in some cases cause allergic reactions.

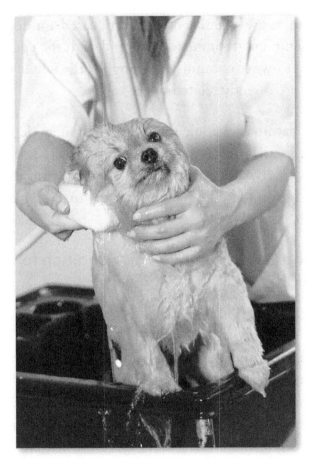

*Quality grooming products nourish and condition
the Pomeranian's coat and skin.*

What is the Best Brush for your Pomeranian?

Brushing your Pomeranian's coat is one of the single most vital processes to maintain a natural sheen, remove dirt and debris, detangle, prevent pelting, control shedding, and promote the good health of the Pom's skin. A good brush and comb are essential to get deeply into the thick coat and gently remove debris, matting, and to stimulate the skin.

For daily brushing a flexible slicker brush is vital. Slicker brushes are effective at getting deep into the coat. A level-2 comb is used to check for tangles and separate the hairs. A finishing brush is needed to smooth the fur and produce a smooth, shiny appearance.

Pomeranian Dog Toys – What Fun and Stimulating Toys are Good for Your Pomeranian?

Providing interesting toys for your Pomeranian affects the overall health, security, development, and even temperament of the dog. Toys keep a Pom engaged, prevent boredom, and in some cases provide comfort. It isn't essential that a dog has an abundance of different toys. It is critical the toys chosen are age and breed appropriate and safe.

Toys for Pomeranians must be of sound construction and free of small parts that may present a swallowing and/or choking hazard.

Plush toys – Plush toys are favorite human gifts for their fur-babies. Many Poms enjoy cuddling and experience companionship and comfort from such toys. Pomeranians are not especially strong chewers, but they can rip into soft, fiber filled, plush toys rather quickly – especially if there is a hidden treasure like a squeaker inside. Sturdier plush toys that are specially designed for dogs are recommended.

Chew toys – Chew toys are not just for Pomeranian puppies; adult dogs also enjoy the activity of chewing on hard-cast nylon or rubber bones. The exercise of chewing also strengthens jaws and cleans teeth.

Treat release toys – Treat release toys are great for the 'home alone' Pom. Treat release toys are usually made from molded nylon or rubber. They have a storage area to hide a treat like kibble, cheese, or peanut butter. A Pomeranian will busy himself in pursuit of the treasure for a long period of time. Make sure the treat-release toy you choose is designed for small breed dogs.

Interactive toys – Balls, disks, agility props, and ropes are among the toys that human and dog can enjoy together. Interactive toys are wonderful tools to increase the bonding experience.

Pomeranian toys should be breed and age-appropriate, and safe.

Pomeranian Puppy Toys – Which toys are age appropriate and safe?

A Pomeranian Puppy goes through teething stages much like a human baby. During these phases, the puppy's gums itch, become sore and often hurt. The discomfort leads the pup to seek out sources that provide comfort. It is during teething stages that a good deal of damage to furniture, doors, steps, shoes, belts, rugs, and other household items occurs. Available toys that soothe the gums and satisfy the urge to chew can be priceless!

Teething toys should be purchased with the tiny Pomeranian Puppy size in mind. Sections of the chew toy should be able to fit in the dog's mouth without the danger of breaking apart and presenting a choking hazard. Chew toys should be pliable but sturdy. Some puppy teething toys are flavored to engage the dog's interest. Most teething toys feature bumps, nubs, or ribs to massage sore, tender gums.

Your Pomeranian Dog's toys should be inspected and rotated on a regular basis. A toy with loose parts, breaks, tears, or sharp edges should be discarded. Toys that become soiled and cannot be cleaned should also be replaced. Giving your Pom a few toys at a time and introducing different toys occasionally will keep him entertained and interested.

Pomeranian Treats – What Treats are Safe and Healthy for Your Pomeranian?

Pomeranians have a reputation for being picky eaters. Make no mistake; a high-value treat is so irresistible; few Poms will turn their cute little nose up at one. Tempting, delicious goodies are effective training tools, but over-consumption of snacks can lead to excessive weight gain and the associated health problems. Treats (aka "doggie junk food") are made from the same basic ingredients as commercially prepared dog food but with a higher content of fat, sugar, sodium, and ultimately calories. It should be recognized treats are not made with high nutritional values in mind, they are made to taste good. Just practice treat moderation – even when training.

Read the labels on packages and choose treats that are high in meat and protein, and lowest in sugar, sodium, and fat. Choose treats that are manufactured in the USA, Canada or countries with production regulations. Smaller bits are best for Pomeranians, especially if the treat is used as a reward for training. Dried meats like jerky are more difficult to chew and swallow easily. Lower calorie, healthier, "natural" treats are available from your pantry or refrigerator. Many dogs like bits of carrots, broccoli, green beans, sweet potatoes, and fruit like blueberries and apples.

Pomeranian Clothes – Should you Dress your Pomeranian?

Canine clothing is big business, especially for toy breeds like the Pomeranian. Dressing the dog for success is hardly a new fad. Portraits of dogs in King Henry III's court feature royal pooches wearing fancy collars of velvet and silk. Clothes may make a fashion statement, but in many cases dressing for the occasion is very practical.

Pomeranian Weather Protective Clothes – Pomeranian Dog Jackets and Sweaters

Pomeranians have very little body fat. Despite that dense, double coat of fur, the little Pom can chill very quickly. Rain, snow, sleet, wind, plain old cold weather will make a Pomeranian reluctant to go outside. Weather appropriate outerwear can make all the difference between a healthy, reliably housebroken, well-exercised Pom and a barking, restless, anxious dog. All weather Pomeranian dog jackets and sweaters are available through most pet-related retail outlets.

The Pomeranian Dog is prone to skin allergies and disorders. Medical treatment for such issues frequently involves the application of ointments and topical lotions. These applications may leave residue on furniture, rugs, and floors. A doggie sweater or shirt may be used to protect the Pom's skin and keep the ointment in place and off areas of the house.

Weather appropriate clothing will keep your
Pom warm and comfortable outside.

Pomeranian Shoes and Boots

The sight of a Pomeranian diva strutting her stuff in a cute pair of snow boots is certainly a show stopper. Shoes and boots for Poms are available in many styles and colors. Certainly, a fashion statement, canine footwear also serves an important purpose. Snowy, icy winter weather often brings out the salt and other chemicals to treat streets and sidewalks. A good pair of boots will protect your Pomeranians feet from the cold and abrasive solvents that may burn, irritate, or damage those little paws. Summer shoes will shield a Pom's sensitive paw pads from hot, burning asphalt, sidewalks, and even the irritation of sand. Be sure to count the shoes or boots upon removal and put them in a safe location out of reach of your Pomeranian or other pets.

Some clothes are just plain fun!

Pomeranian Just for Fun Clothes – Dresses, Buttons, Bows, and Tiaras

There are practical reasons for dressing your Pom, but there are also reasons for picking up that little black doggie dress, a 'look at me' bow, feathered boa, or the bling of a tiara – the biggest of which is FUN! Nothing is cuter than a fluffy, teddy-bear of a Pomeranian wearing high-style. It is undeniable that most

Poms like nothing more than being the center of attention. An audience of smiles, laughs, applause, requests for photo-ops, hugs, kisses, or a much-appreciated random treat for the well-dressed Pom is the ultimate pay off. Go ahead, pamper your prince or princess and shop the many catalogs of divine dresses and accessories for the well-dressed Pomeranian!

CHAPTER 7

Pomeranian Training – How to Get Started Training and Succeed

L iving with a Pomeranian Dog is a gratifying experience. The Pom's natural enthusiasm, grace, affection, and forgiveness provides valuable life-lessons for the entire family. A mannerly, polite dog is a joy for its family and its community but adapting to the expectations of the human world is learned.

A well-trained dog participates with the family; he goes on trips, greets guests, and plays with kids. A Pomeranian good citizen is a trusted, welcomed companion and a beloved neighbor in the community, thanks to his or her exemplary behavior. Studies indicate training is the number one reason a dog remains in a "forever" home, versus ending up in a shelter. In the event a dog has to be surrendered, training can mean the difference in rehoming or death.

Training develops strong lines of communication. It provides the best tool for establishing a bond, building trust, enhancing the human/canine relationship, and it enriches the life you share with the best friend you could ever have.

Pomeranian Dog Training – At what age should a Pomeranian Training Program start?

The appropriate age to begin training your Pomeranian Dog is the minute you lift him or her into your arms. Conditioning starts with that initial connection. Training is a form of communication, and when you hold your Pom, regardless of his age you speak the universal language of love. Even a tiny puppy understands, *"I love you, you are safe, I promise to protect you."*

An effective training program should be considered at each stage of your Pomeranian's development. Plan your program and work your plan. As you train your dog, you expand your means of communication. Courses should be safe, fun, and enjoyable. Exercise patience, affection, and persistence at all times.

Training should be fun, safe, and consistent.

What are the Proper Pomeranian Training Techniques?

Training may extend from teaching a puppy how to live in their human's home to teaching impressive, elaborate tricks and entertaining performance routines. Regardless of the ultimate goal, a successful training program begins with developing a four-legged family member that understands and obeys the household rules.

Training Basics – Firm and Consistent Training

The rate of training success depends on establishing a solid foundation and consistent communications. Plan to train, beginning the first day your Pomeranian Dog arrives in his or her new home. Try to hold training sessions at the same time every day (before a meal is a great time as the dog will be most attentive — especially if food lures are used).

To optimize the learning experience, training sessions should be fun and exciting. Do not create a stressful environment. If you are frustrated, weary, rushed for time, or if your Pom exhibits a difficult time concentrating; relax, calm down, and start again. It isn't necessary to learn a new task every day; it is necessary to stay on track by working your time schedule and exercising learned skills on a daily basis.

Choose a training area that is relatively free from distractions to begin. It is most difficult to gain your puppy's attention if a group of children or other dogs are playing nearby.

The four critical steps to follow when teaching a successful training task are

1. **Request**
2. **Lure**
3. **Response**
4. **Reward**

Sounds simple, and it can be. Pomeranians learn fast. Most trainers recommend a three-pass goal. Accomplish a task successfully three times in a row, and your dog will reliably repeat the task, on command.

Operant Conditioning — A basic technique in dog training involves operant conditioning. Essentially, operant conditioning works on the principle that behavior is the product of the consequence. In other words, your dog carries out an action because of what happens after he does it.

You issue the command *"sit,"* and your dog obeys —you provide a treat and a hearty *"good boy."* You give the command *"sit,"* and your dog enthusiastically jumps up on you in search of a treat — you say, *"NO,"* and turn away. Both situations represent an example of operant conditioning. Practicing operant conditioning rewards your dog when he carries out a command successfully or punishes him for undesired behavior by withholding what he seeks. Each result builds reinforcement of an action with an appropriate response. The operant condition is considered the easiest and most effective technique to shape behavior.

Under no circumstances should a training program involve punitive, physical punishment, or abuse. Physically hitting, kicking, or other violent actions only frighten the dog and breaks the trust bond with the trainer. Your goal is to establish healthy respect and obedience — not establish fear and anxiety.

Pomeranian Treats – What are Good Treats for Positive Reinforcement?

A Pomeranian may be a people pleaser, but when it comes to training, it becomes quickly apparent the way to a dog's heart (or head), is through his stomach. Most dogs will do nearly anything for the right reward. A consistent training program should depend on a variety of rewards-not just yummy food treats.

Food treats provide a quick way to get your dog's immediate attention. Food is an immediate, pleasing payoff for the desired behavior. Positive rewards teach the meaning of a command and reinforce successful consequences.

Even the most sought-after delights can lose their appeal. To avoid reward fatigue, add values to the treat system. Anything your dog reacts positively toward can be used as a lure. You may rank your reward system to include

- High-value treats; pieces of meat, cheese, bits of favorite dog biscuits.
- Treats; pieces of kibble or dog food, chunks of apples, sweet potatoes.
- Verbal rewards; *good boy/good girl.*
- Affection rewards; pat the head, scratch an ear.

Master trainers recommend following the 'half dozen rule'; only use food for a half dozen command trials. As soon as the dog is reliably able to execute the exercise, phase out the food and begin to use hand signals or audible cues for reinforcement. Developing the secondary reinforcement system and phasing out food treats is highly recommended for a healthy, successful training program.

How to Train your Pomeranian – What are the Training Skills every Pomeranian Should Learn?

Training your dog to behave appropriately is like teaching your children good manners. It makes them a pleasure to be around, it reduces damage to your property, and it keeps your Pom safer. The Pomeranian is an exceptionally intelligent breed. This trait makes them very easy to train. Some owners may have visions of obedience medals; others may want to show off their dog (and their own training skills) to family and friends by teaching a routine of impressive tricks. Regardless of the ambition, there are training skills every Pomeranian should learn.

The most important word your Pom will learn is **"NO."** It is a natural command, and they learn it early on. Always speak with authority and make sure your pup understands you mean it when you say **"NO!"** Give him zero alternatives — **"NO"** means **"NO!"** When you say **"NO"** going forward with the activity must result in undesirable circumstances. Someday the **"NO"** command could save your Pomeranian's life.

Train yourself to deliver the **"NO"** message in a consistent manner. Softening your tone, allowing variety in messaging, and not administering a negative result every time, will tend to confuse the puppy and complicate the training. If you fail to establish rules and enforce them, your Pom will make his or her own!

Remember, a Pomeranian can be stubborn with a penchant for getting his own way. Despite the breed specific tendency, this little dog is wholeheartedly interested in earning his human's approval, and a high-value yummy treat goes a long way toward reinforcing good, learned behavior.

Teach the entire family and occasional visitors to observe the house rules. It isn't fair to allow your Pomeranian on the couch when Uncle Bud visits, and then reprimand her for jumping on the furniture the rest of the time.

Potty training is at the top of the list of training priorities.

Pomeranian Potty Training

No doubt potty training your new family member is at the top of the "must do" list of activities. Housetraining a Pomeranian may seem like an insurmountable task. They can — and will — go anywhere! Keep your objective in perspective. You are attempting to accomplish only two goals;

- Prevent urination and defecation in unacceptable areas.
- Reinforce urination and defecation in designated areas.

Housetraining your Pomeranian requires initiating the practice of 5 P's

- **PLAN**
- **PROCESS**
- **PREVENTION**
- **PERSEVERANCE**
- **PATIENCE**

Bear in mind, until a Pomeranian Puppy reaches 12 weeks of age he/she cannot control their bladder. Most puppies will dribble urine as they walk or run and cannot "hold it," until they reach their designated potty spot. That consideration is not to suggest housetraining should be delayed, but there are certain limitations during the early stages of potty training.

Work the housetraining plan around your dog's eating, sleeping, and playing routine. Keep your Pom on a consistent feeding schedule. Take food away between meals. As soon as your dog eats it is time to go "potty." Introduce the verbal command of choice for 'going' and use it when you feel it is time for your dog's elimination breaks.

Immediately upon finishing a meal, waking up, playing, or drinking, attach your Pomeranian's leash and say your cue word. It may be best to carry the dog outside or to the puppy pad to avoid accidents. Set her in the designated area and repeat the cue word. Keep the dog in place until she has successfully eliminated. Praise her efforts — this is a training action that may not require a food treat. Simply making a celebration out of the success is enough to establish positive reinforcement.

Where to go?

The first decision of a successful housetraining plan is where to establish the potty spot. Should you train the dog to go inside or outside? Most owners hope to train their puppies with dual options. Having a designated area inside the house is important if you are away for long periods and cannot get back to take the dog outside on a schedule.

Inside — There are several reasons to train a Pomeranian to eliminate in a designated area inside. Urban dwellers without easy access to green spaces need an inside potty space. Pomeranian Dogs are physically fragile and may be adversely affected by cold weather. Depending on the living conditions you may need to establish an inside potty area exclusively.

The training principals for inside potty space versus outside are essentially the same, though tools may vary a bit. Instead of a grass surface as the 'go' trigger, you will potty train on puppy pads, newspapers, or a litter box. There are products designed to stimulate a dog's instinctive urge to eliminate.

The first step is to establish a specific potty place that is easy to clean, and preferably not carpeted. A space close to an outside door works well, especially if you plan to train for dual inside/outside facilities.

Designate an area that is about 3-4 square feet. Use ONLY that one area. Multiple inside locations will prove confusing for the dog. Commit to the best potty tool based on your lifestyle:

- **Puppy pads** are easy to use, disposable, layered pads. The base layer is designed to be leak-proof and holds urine in to protect floors. The top layer consists of woven fibers treated with an attractant such as horse urine to cue the dog's elimination.

- **Litter boxes** are containers designed to hold cat litter, shredded newspapers, or sand. Spray attractants are available to stimulate the dog's interest in and use of the litter box.

- **Newspapers** may work like puppy pads in theory. They are not as absorbent and do not offer the protection of multiple layers like a puppy pad. Training to newspapers may cause the dog to consider ANY newspaper a viable place to potty.

Avoid using towels and rugs as a potty pad. The Pom will never reliably distinguish the difference between an old rug suitable for potty and a priceless heirloom carpet.

Watch carefully. When your dog seems agitated, walks around in circles or begins sniffing the floor, take her to the potty place. It is advisable to use a leash to prevent wandering from the designated potty spot inside or outside. As soon as she is successful, reward her with positive rewards. Make sure she knows you are pleased with her success.

When potty accidents occur — and they will — do not punish. As soon as you see your puppy in "the act" pick her up, and correct her in a firm voice. Keep repeating the verbal command as you place her in the designated location. If she finishes eliminating in her potty place, praise and reward. Never rub your dog's nose in the urine or feces. When you've discovered an accident but did not catch her in the act, it is too late to correct. Simply clean up, watch, and wait for the next opportunity.

Inside housetraining is often easier for Pomeranians than for other breeds. Still, the process may take longer because of the numerous opportunities for accidents. Confined spaces and crates assist housebreaking efforts by keeping the Pom from straying to hidden areas.

Some dogs trained for inside elimination are never able to achieve success outside. Be sure to keep an enzymatic, urine/stool neutralizer on hand, and clean areas of accidents thoroughly. Dogs will return to a soiled area bearing the scent of previous accidents.

Outside — Pomeranian owners who prefer an outside potty spot will train their puppy for cues to go out. It is natural for a dog to eliminate outside, so developing an outdoor system maximizes an inherent trait.

Choose the designated potty place relatively close to the door. Plan to take your puppy outside about every two hours during the initial training. Clearly establish the routine: potty first - then play. Immediately go to the potty space and stay there until the dog is successful. Praise, reward, then go for a walk or play.

Prepare to get up at least once a night to take your Pom out. They can wait a bit longer at night while sleeping, they do not eat or drink, and they are less active.

If you are planning indoor/outdoor potty options, keep puppy pads or a litter box next to the exit door. As your puppy becomes reliable at using the pads or litter box, graduate to taking her outside when she appears ready to go potty. You should accomplish inside training, before adding outside training.

How to deal with Negative Pomeranian Behavior?

Pomeranians are diminutive, teddy-bear-like adorable animals. They are totally charming, cuddly, and cute. They inspire the human impulse to coddle and pamper. Still, this lovely little dog is a canine and subject to the survival instincts and tendencies of their ancestry.

Before domestication, dogs lived in the wild. Their very existence depended on the ability to hunt, hide, protect, and procreate. In the human world, many of their survival instincts are simply not suitable for household harmony. As the pack leader, you must learn what behavior is acceptable, and what intervention is required for unacceptable, destructive, and perhaps dangerous actions.

Aggressive Pomeranians – Should Aggression be a Concern?

Examine the personalities of puppies within a single litter, and you will discover dominant Pomeranians and submissive Poms. A dominant Pom also called an alpha, may exercise a leadership role that extends beyond the litter and into the new family environment. There is a difference between a dominant/alpha dog, and an aggressive dog. The distinction must be made to determine the appropriate course of corrective action.

Pomeranians by nature are divas. They crave the center stage. They can be dramatic and jealous of attention shifts. Poms also have the need to control their home and possessions, which includes their human. They have a strong personality and can be manipulative. Pompoms are often perceived as "pint-sized bullies."

Dominant dogs will bark, growl, mouth, or nip during play. They are cautious but curious. They may paw, bat, or pounce on playmates or toys. An alpha dog will want to stay with his human, and often become protective, but will back down when assured of safety.

An aggressive dog is subject to snarling, growling, lunging, snapping, biting, and fighting. The actions can be triggered any number of things like perceived threats, invasion of space, fear, anxiety, the potential loss of favorite toys or food.

It is normal for dogs to yip, grumble, and growl to communicate and establish pack order and status. It is not normal for a dog to express aggressive behavior toward another pet, or person. In such circumstances, immediately remove the dog from the situation, use the **"NO"** command, and if possible crate or sequester him.

Aggression in any dog is dangerous. Talk with your veterinarian about possible causes and appropriate treatment. Consulting a behavior specialist for an intervention therapy plan may be necessary.

Excessive Pomeranian Barking

Dogs bark! It is their way of communicating. Some dogs bark more than others. In the canine world, Pomeranians are the reigning champs of barking. They feel it is essential to tell you about every sight, sound, scent, or subtle change in the environment. Shelter volunteers report "barking" as the primary reason cited by owners surrendering their Pomeranian for rehoming. The propensity to bark is certainly a consideration when evaluating the Pomeranian Dog as the right pet for your family.

While some barking is expected, the excessive bark – even for the Pomeranian — may be minimized by redirecting with training. There are five tips to help reduce your Pomeranian's desire to bark.

1. Remove the motivation. If your dog is barking at activity outside the window or door, close or cover the window. If he is in the yard, bring him inside.
2. Teach the "quiet" command. Encourage your Pom to "speak." Offer a treat when he barks. When he stops barking to smell the treat, praise, and reward. He will soon understand it is

the act of stopping that results in a treat. Add the "quiet" command as he becomes more reliable with the "speak" training.

3. Distract your barking Pom with a command that is not compatible with barking. Show her a treat while giving a "sit" or "down" command.

4. Provide your Pomeranian with plenty of exercise and mental stimulation. A tired, satisfied dog is less likely to exert the effort to bark excessively.

5. Ignore the barking. Dogs receive some satisfaction from reprimands. Any attention is positive attention in their book. When your dog barks, walk away, go to another room, make sure he understands you are not interested in his vocalizing.

Keep the desensitizing training fun and upbeat. Don't yell at a barking dog, it only adds to the commotion. Be consistent; nothing will work the first time, commit to a technique and use it over and over until the desired results are obtained.

Training for Pomeranian Socialization

The Pomeranian is an extremely social breed. The little dogs literally crave social interaction. Without exposure to people, other animals, and public environments they can become fearful, timid, aggressive, and develop other serious behavioral problems.

To socialize your Pom, expose him or her to a variety of people, animals, places, sounds, smells, and other objects. Always provide him with a safe, controlled setting when initiating new experiences. Use positive rewards to reinforce positive reactions.

Remain calm in each setting. Allow your Pomeranian to explore, if he appears fearful encourage investigation. Do not remove him immediately, teach him to "settle."

Start each experience slowly and build. Take her along on regular errands. Go to the dry cleaners, drive through banks or food takeout windows, stop by a playground, and visit pet-friendly retail stores. Encourage strangers to touch, pet, and admire at will. As your Pomeranian puppy becomes more comfortable with new places mix up the environments. It is especially important to expose her to the veterinarian's office, groomer, or boarding kennel before she requires treatment to make her more comfortable and manageable when she does go there.

Experts suggest introducing at least 100 new people and experiences to your Pom during his first six months. Dogs that are well-socialized are happier, healthier, and much better canine citizens.

Training a Pomeranian to Swim – Can a Pomeranian be conditioned to Love the Water?

Pomeranians are not known for their proclivity for water. Their foundation breeds were no "water dogs." Surprisingly, even dog breeds that are "water dogs" do not swim naturally, they must be taught. Given that bit of information, there is hope you can teach a Pom to swim, loving the water may be another matter.

Like their human counterparts, some dogs have a natural affection for the water. Swimming seems to come easy, and they will eagerly jump and swim away at the least opportunity. It is a great skill to teach, you never know when your little Pom may fall in a pool, a pond, even the bathtub and need to swim for his life!

Make the bath the first introduction to water. A bath should be a safe, controlled, and pleasurable experience. If your Pom has a traumatic encounter in the tub, you can bet teaching him to swim will be a good deal more difficult.

If the bathtub proves satisfactory, move your Pom up to another controlled body of water. A small kiddie pool is a good next step. Fill the pool so the dog can stand, without submerging his head. Use favorite toys as incentives to move about in the pool.

Always have your Pomeranian wear a life jacket in the water,
even if he is an excellent swimmer.

Allow your Pomeranian to approach larger bodies of water such as streams, ponds, or swimming pools as he deems comfortable. If you or other family members are in the pool, encourage your Pom to join you. Be ready to carry the dog in until you are certain of the swimming ability. Never leave a dog unattended in the water. Do not let them tire with too much activity. Offer high-value rewards for accomplishment. It is recommended to use a life jacket for a Pomeranian, even if he or she proves to be an accomplished swimmer. Do not be discouraged if your Pom does not embrace swimming. She will happily stay on dry land and cheer the efforts of the family's water games.

CHAPTER 8

Pomeranian Dog Health – What Should You Know

The lifespan of a healthy Pom can exceed 16 years! A healthy, robust, energetic Pomeranian is a joy. Several elements contribute to the overall health of a canine – genetics, nutrition, exercise, and routine medical care. Keeping your Pom healthy should be an utmost priority. Understanding the components of health will help ensure your fur-child enjoys a lifetime of wellness.

Your veterinarian is your healthy Pomeranian's best friend.

Pomeranian Health Concerns – What are the Common Problems for this Breed?

As a breed Pomeranians are sturdy dogs with limited health issues. Provided with a balanced diet, preventative healthcare, appropriate exercise, and good grooming, a well-bred Pom should experience limited physical problems.

Genetic Conditions

All dog breeds have some genetic propensity for disease. That does not mean your Pomeranian will have any of the common problems associated with their breed. A conscientious breeder will screen mating pairs for identifiable congenital conditions, before breeding. A dog carrying a gene that may produce a physical deficiency in the offspring should be removed from the breeding program. The following hereditary conditions are identified most commonly in the Pomeranian Dog.

Pomeranian Alopecia – Is a condition that contributes to hair loss on a part or all of the Pomeranian's body. *Black Skin Disease* is a common disorder that is prevalent when hyperpigmentation combines with Pomeranian alopecia. Signs your dog is experiencing alopecia include abnormally heavy shedding and thinning hair.

Pomeranian Ametropia – Is a condition that affects the eyesight. Pomeranian ametropia symptoms may be difficult to easily recognize and include double vision, blurred vision, and headaches.

Pomeranian Microphthalmia – Is a condition that affects the eyes. Symptoms of Pomeranian microphthalmia may include abnormally small eyes, eyes that turn inward or crossed eyes.

Pomeranian Colobomas – A hole in a section of the eye such as the retina, iris, choroid, or optic disc is the result of Pomeranian colobomas. In some cases, surgery may be an appropriate treatment for the condition.

Pomeranian Joint Issues – Thanks to the small physical structure of the Pomeranian dog, joint issues are not as common as those experienced in larger breeds. Pomeranians frequently suffer from patellar luxation, a condition of the knee joint. Severe cases of luxating patella can cause lameness and may require surgery.

Pomeranian Collapsing Trachea – Is a common threat among toy dogs. Symptoms include coughing spasms, shallow breathing, gagging, a frequent "honking" cough, or coughing up mucus. In some cases, the Pom may faint due to insufficient air flow. Once thought to be a genetic issue, research now suggests collapsing trachea could be the result of metabolic deficiencies. Tracheal collapse may also be the result of trauma.

Pomeranian Nutrition

Pomeranians often experience health issues related to nutrition. The areas to consider include:

Maintaining Pomeranian Optimal Weight -- Poms are famous for being picky eaters. Owners often resort to feeding anything the dog will eat – good or bad food -- which can result in improper nutritional balance, and obesity. The responsibility of weight control is entirely up to you – the owner. Other Pomeranian weight issues include heart disease, liver disease, digestive disorders, diabetes, shortness of breath, and patellar luxation.

A Pomeranian Dog's weight control is the complete responsibility of the owner.

Eating too fast is another common complaint. Choking, bloating, and other disorders may result from gulping food too quickly. A premium, balanced diet is important for proper body development, appearance, stamina, and overall enhanced health. For your Pomeranian's welfare, it is critical to keep him, or her, fit and trim.

Vitamins for Pomeranian Dogs – Which supplements will most aid your Pomeranian's health? A balanced diet and proper exercise should provide your Pomeranian with all of the nutritional requirements for good health. As your dog ages, or in the event of other physical ailments, your veterinarian may recommend vitamins to manage certain conditions. A canine's needs are very different from humans, and any supplement should be discussed with a qualified medical provider.

Pomeranian Exercise

The Pomeranian dog is small but energetic. This toy breed is a popular pet for many reasons, but perhaps his limited requirements for exercise is a top consideration. While the little Pom does not need as much of a workout as larger dogs, he does need a short daily walk or two, a romp around an enclosed space, or a brisk, physical game like fetch to keep him mentally stimulated and healthy.

Pomeranian Preventative Healthcare

Your trusted veterinarian will become your healthy Pomeranian's best friend. Regular medical examinations can prevent many dangerous diseases. They can also minimize treatment if a condition is identified early.

Pomeranian vaccinations – Inoculating your Pomeranian against infectious, life-threatening diseases, is a vital element in health care. Every year as a part of the annual health check, vaccination protocols are administered by your vet. The threat of diseases such as rabies, distemper, parvovirus, hepatitis, Bordetella (kennel cough), leptospirosis, coronavirus, Lyme disease, and many parasites is minimized or eliminated as a result of regular vaccines. The type of vaccine, dosage, and frequency is often based on regional conditions. Your veterinarian will recommend which inoculations your Pom should receive.

Pomeranian health examinations –A regular examination by a qualified healthcare provider should be scheduled on an annual basis. In addition to weight and growth measurements, your veterinarian should conduct a thorough assessment of your Pomeranian's

--Coat and skin

--Chest, heart, and lungs

--Eyes, ears, mouth, teeth, and gums

--Abdomen

--Joints

--Stool (to check for parasites).

You should be prepared to discuss diet, eating, elimination, exercise, behavior, and any concerns you may have regarding your dog's health. A comprehensive healthcare program is a key to overall Pomeranian wellness.

Pomeranian Grooming

A Pomeranian is admired for his or her coat, bright eyes, bushy tail, curiosity, and energy. Many of those attributes are dependent on a consistent grooming program. Grooming goes beyond brushing and combing all of that lovely fur. It carries benefits that contribute to good health.

Pomeranian tooth loss – A common threat to Pomeranians is created by retained baby teeth, which can lead to an improper bite and tooth loss. Daily brushing and checking the teeth and gums can identify problems early.

Pomeranian severe hair loss syndrome – Daily brushing keeps the coat shiny and is the best defense for shedding. Brushing stimulates the skin. It provides a tool to determine other serious conditions such as fleas, mange, Cushing's disease, alopecia, black skin disease, and hyperpigmentation.

Pomeranian ear health – Regular ear care should be a part of your grooming program. Ears should be kept clean and free of wax and debris. The skin should be a healthy color (not red and irritated). Cut away excess hair inside the canal and around the ear flaps. Cleaning will prevent painful infections.

Pomeranian eye health – The Pomeranian's eyes should be washed with a cotton ball and warm water. Excessive tearing or staining may indicate infections or other conditions and should be checked by a veterinarian.

Pomeranian nail care – Trimming your Pomeranian's toenails should be done every two weeks. If the nails grow too long, they are more difficult to cut. Long nails can get caught and tear causing a painful injury. Long nails can impair your Pom's ability or interest in exercise and may contribute to lameness.

CHAPTER 9

Pomeranian Dogs
Around the World

Today, Pomeranian Dogs are found in every country in the world. From royal courts to celebrity purses, to the porches, patios, and parlors of everyday folks, the darling divas earn their position as one of the most popular dog breeds on earth. Pom fanatics love to love their favored pets. Many owner's interests contain an obsession with all things Pomeranian. As a result, products of every size, shape, color, and service are available featuring…what else? Pomeranians!!

Gifts for the Pomeranian Lover

Purses, paintings, photos, even lollipops representing loveable Pomeranian Dogs are available in any number of product catalogs and retail outlets. An Internet search of the words "Pomeranian Gifts" will return a page of options from extravagant, expensive items to basic do-it-yourself ideas. Among the popular gifts for Pomeranian lovers are:

Pomeranian coffee cup – Could anything be better than sipping a favorite drink with your favorite mug on the mug? Coffee cups bearing the resemblance of a Pomeranian in any variety of colors are offered for sale online at sites such as Amazon and eBay.

Pomeranian shirt – Wear your love for your Pomeranian proudly. A shirt emblazoned with the face of your favorite pooch screams affection. Internet marketers like Etsy, Zazzle, Amazon, and eBay advertise a wide variety of human apparel featuring Pomeranians. Many animal rescue organizations also sell breed-specific apparel, as a fundraising tool.

Pomeranian ornaments – The American Kennel Club Marketplace offer Pomeranian ornaments. Decorate for the holidays or displayed year-round, these ornaments are whimsical, clever, cute, and fun…much like their inspiration!

Other cool gift ideas for the Pomeranian aficionado include calendars, jewelry, pillows, umbrellas, totes, lunch bags, clocks, keyrings, plush, notepads, coloring books, blankets, snow globes, shoes, greeting cards, and dinner plates.

*Cool gifts for the Pomeranian lover include
notepads, greeting cards, and coloring books!*

CHAPTER 10

The Proper Pomeranian Mix – What are the Popular "Designer" Pomeranian Mixed Breeds?

You have your heart set on a Pomeranian, another family member wants a Pug, how to find a balance? Perhaps with a mixed breed – ½ Pom and ½ Pug, a Pomerpug! The creative art of "designer breed" dogs has captured the imagination of breeders and pet owners alike.

The Proper Pomeranian Mix – What Are the Popular "Designer" Pomeranian Mixed Breeds?

While breed purists frown on the concept, creating cleverly mixed breed dogs is becoming a worldwide phenomenon, think Labradoodle! Some of the more popular Pom mixes include

- **Pomsky** – A mix of a Pomeranian and Husky.
- **Pomchi** – A mix of a Pomeranian and Chihuahua.
- **Shiranian** – A mix of a Pomeranian and Shitzu.

- **Pomapoo** – A mix of a Pomeranian and Poodle.

- **Yorkie-Pom or Porkie** – A mix of a Pomeranian and Yorkshire Terrier.

- **Maltipom** – A mix of Pomeranian and Maltese

Designer breeds like this Pomeranian+Poodle mix have captured the creativity interest of breeders and fans alike.

One man's mutt may be another man's one-of-a-kind specialty. Designer breeds lack the consistency of purebred dogs (which explains how they can be one-of-a-kind). Even in the same litter, two different breed dogs can produce a variety of physically unique puppies. Serious breeders would never intentionally mate two purebred dogs of different breeds. Still, the interest (and subsequent demand) in designer dogs is certainly growing. Bear in mind, adopting a "hybrid" or mixed breed dog does not guarantee a dog with predictable traits. Some advocates will argue crossing a Pomeranian with a toy Poodle will create an intelligent, non-shedding, tiny dog. This is not necessarily true. The genetics may dictate the size of the animal, as the only trait carried over (assuming both mating breeds are physically small). Crossbreeding increases the population of mixed breed dogs, adding to the burden of unwanted dogs abandoned to shelters. Kennel clubs like the International Designer Canine Registry (IDCR) are dedicated to maintaining a database of the various mixed, 'designer' breeds.

Conclusion

Pomeranians are among the most popular purebred dogs on earth. Since the Victorian era, the desirable attributes of the Pomeranian have been cultivated to create a charming, hearty, intelligent, beautiful companion animal. Pomeranians grace royal courts, charm the rich and famous, and provide comfort and unconditional love to families around the world. People are enchanted by the Pom's teddy-bear appearance, and animated, cheerful personality. Their versatile, compact, little bodies make them easy to transport nearly anywhere with their human. Poms are trainable, polite, and they make excellent lap dogs, service dogs, show dogs, therapy dogs, as well as many other enviable roles.

Pomeranians are not for everyone. They require daily grooming to maintain that luxurious coat. They are robust and spunky, yet fragile. They can be easily injured. A Pom living with small children can be problematic. They really love to bark. Among dogs, they are considered the canine busybody, striving to shout out everyone's comings and goings! Pomeranians are also notoriously stubborn and can develop a serious Napoleon Complex, if not trained correctly.

Their charm wins the day, however, and Pomeranian devotees cannot imagine another dog they would prefer to their precious Pom fur-child.

Pomeranians leave big footprints on the human heart.

A Pomeranian can adjust to nearly any type home, as long as she is the center of attention. The most significant requirement of a good Pom owner is the commitment to love and care for the dog for life.

Potential Pomeranian owners should learn everything they can about the breed. Understanding the time, labor, health care, training, and attention a Pom requires, goes a long way toward ensuring a good transition and a happy forever home. You can be sure your Pomeranian will leave big footprints on your heart – for life!

Your Trusted Pomeranian Resource List

Breeders of Pomeranians / Breeder Directories (USA)

- *The American Pomeranian Club*
  http://www.americanpomeranianclub.org
  Pomeranian Foundation club of American Kennel Club.
  Provides a sanctioned breeder listing by US State.
- *Char's Pomeranians*
  http://www.charspoms.com – USA Breeder,
  AKC Breeder of Merit
  Bark River, Michigan
- *Lynnwrightpoms.com* – USA Breeder,
  https://www.lynnwrightpoms.com/
  Bel Air, Maryland, breeds for health and temperament
- *YKnot Pomeranians* – USA Breeder
  http://yknotpoms.com/
  La Plata, Maryland

- *Velocity Pomeranians*
  http://www.velocityshowdogs.com USA Breeder,
  Specializes in Show Quality Pomeranians
  Brooklyn, New York

Breeders of Pomeranians (Canada)

- *Bonsai Pomeranians*
  https://www.bonsaipoms.com- Canada Breeder,
  Pomeranians are CKC and AKC registered
  Hamilton, Ontario
- *Kristari Pomeranians*
  http://www.kristari.com – Canada Breeder
  CKC Lifetime member
  Southern Ontario

Breeders of Pomeranians (Europe)

- *The Kennel Club – United Kingdom*
  https://www.thekennelclub.org.uk/
  Features list of Kennel Club "Assured Breeders" throughout
  Europe

Pomeranian Rescue Groups

- *Rescue Me!*
  http://pomeranian.rescueme.org/
  Not for profit organization providing free listings for
  Pomeranian shelters, rescues, and foster homes.

Made in the USA
Coppell, TX
25 September 2020

38786064R00075